A Grateful Journey

By

Howard E. Marchie, B. H. B.

Artwork

By

Pat Foster

Thanks for the Help

H E Marchie

A Grateful Journey
By
Howard E. Marchie
E-mail   emmarchie@yahoo.com

First Edition
Copyright © 2003

ISBN 0-9728909-9-8

Printed in the United States of America

DEDICATION

To Annie & William Cote
Without you I could never have been

Acknowledgments

Throughout this book you will find many people alluded to but rarely named. Not using their names relieved my anxiety about violating their privacy. Many of the people involved in this grateful journey have since passed away. I have often regretted my inability to express gratitude to them in a more profound way while they lived. I can only hope that they were aware of my progress and understood that they had played an important role in my development.

When I was discharged from the Air Force I began to renew old friendships made in civilian life. When friends learned that I had been accepted at Fitchburg State they were stunned. Our education and societal directions never pointed in that direction. We were all to become working class people. Most of us rarely wore a suit and never owned more than two ties. They did not know that their disbelief worked as a tremendous confidence-building tool for me and I dared not fail the challenge.

The first people I would like to acknowledge are my birth mother who gave me life and had the good sense in those difficult times to let the Massachusetts Child Welfare Department finance and oversee my development. Their good judgment resulted in my placement with William and Anne Cote whom I recognize as my true parents and who provided the love and nurturing necessary to all children.

When finally deciding to pen this journey that was first suggested by my son-in-law, Philip Visser, I started research at the Massachusetts State House accompanied by close friends, Pat and Dick Foster. Pat Foster is a highly regarded New England artist. She also developed the artwork displayed on the cover. Thanks, Pat.

We had difficulty finding out how to access my records at the state house. A friendly security guard directed us to the Office of the Secretary of State. I tentatively opened the office door and was greeted warmly. An aide asked us to wait while she made a few calls to ascertain the direction we should take. She returned with the name of one of the workers in the welfare office on Washington Street. From there calls were made to the Social Services Department on

Farnsworth Street where we met Helen Cameron-Mahoney who conducted the search of the archives and retrieved the data needed to reconstruct the first eighteen years of my existence.

Thanks to my family, William, Justin, Andrea, and Brandon who along with their mother, my wife, shared in the greater part of this journey. Special thanks given to the editor-in-chief/wife that deciphered my written thoughts and deftly put them into proper form. Both she and I are grateful to our sons and daughter who understand computers and solved problems when queried. There are others who influenced my direction in life. Among them was Walter Markham, my high school principal who initially introduced the idea of a college education to me as well as the staff at Fitchburg State College that helped implement that goal.

I had support along the way from friends who have no idea how much they contributed to this journey. There was my boyhood protagonist, Mike O'Neil and friends such as Jimmy Banks and Jerry Fitzgerald along with long time friends, Jack Lynch and Bill and Sylvia Kane who opened my eyes to a variety of experiences I may never have known.

Prologue

I have never been one to ponder the events that led to my existence. About my birth parents I knew nothing and had not the slightest curiosity about them.

My earliest recollection of the beginning of life seems to go back no further than the age of three. As a ward of the state of Massachusetts, I had the unbelievable good fortune of being placed in the foster care of the Cotes. They were the only parents I would ever acknowledge throughout my life. They and I were solely responsible for who I am, where I went and how I got there up until the time I joined the USAF at the age of eighteen.

It is only recently that my interest has peaked. I have known since about the age of twelve that I have three sisters. They lived as a family unit with different foster parents. Remarkably we lived in the small town of Chelmsford, Massachusetts about five miles apart but never met. More on that later.

When I joined the Air Force, the state department sent me my birth certificate. My name had always been Howard William Marshie {with an s}. The name on the document read Howard Edgerton Marchie {with a c}. I was devastated. How was I to explain this to friends? I have always been a poor speller! Now I couldn't even spell my own name! It turned out to be a minor problem as no one knew or cared about my middle name or theirs. The transposition of an s to a c went unnoticed. It was, however, disconcerting. It became more confounding when I recently became interested in recording my life experiences.

Several years ago while visiting friends in Boston, my wife and I tried to establish contact with the state agency that could provide access to my records while I was a ward of the state {1932-1950}. I tried several phone numbers that appeared to be appropriate. Each time I got an extensive phone menu; nothing seemed applicable. Not knowing how to proceed, we dropped the idea. Another year passed. On a recent visit with our friends, we wandered into the State House hoping to find an information center. There was none. I approached a friendly looking guard and presented my query. He pondered and recommended I try the Office of the Secretary of State. I gasped noting my sandal-shod feet and wrinkled shorts. Not to worry he opined. I didn't.

Upon meekly opening door to the office, we were greeted warmly by the staff. Sighing with relief, I explained our quest. After researching the problem, we were given the names of those who could help us and we went merrily on our way. After meetings in two offices across town, we met with a social service worker who knew precisely what archives to access. She asked for our patience and requested that she be contacted personally if we hadn't heard from her in a month. We did. She apologized. She had tried several avenues with no success. She would keep trying. She had located everyone in the foster home except myself. Two weeks later I called her. No luck, I was aware that the name Marshefsky was my father's name and somehow had been shortened. Bingo! She unearthed twenty-two pages of data.

It is from this information that I have constructed the early stages of my life.

Chapter One

A Dubious Start

By the time of the accident of nature that resulted in my birth on April 14th 1932, my birth parent had already lost three daughters to foster care.

There is no doubt that we were born during difficult times. I have no knowledge of the circumstances in my parents' lives at that time but it is easy to speculate that their existence was not predicated on ease or success.

My sisters appear to be the progeny of Alice Pauline and Bernard Marshefsky. What happened to that union is unknown. My sister, Helen, remembers frequent visits from her father and less often ones with her mother when she first entered foster care. These visits were welcome but ended rather abruptly. The three girls were eventually placed in the same foster home and raised as family unit for many years. My knowledge of my own existence before age three is a non-issue as I remember nothing. What little information I rely on is from several sources. These include my birth certificate from the city of Malden, records recovered from the archives of Social

Services, and from the few tidbits of information from my sister, Helen and my foster mother who was always in communication with the state caseworker.

According to the birth certificate issued by the city of Malden, I was born on April 14,1932. The birth took place in a third story apartment at 16 Clement St. My name was recorded as Howard Edgerton Marchie. My parents' names were listed as Leo Marchie of Brooklyn NY and Margaret {maiden name Foster} of Yarmouth, Nova Scotia, Canada. These names differ from their married names of Bernard and Alice Pauline Marshefsky.

To further complicate the issue of names, state records show that when I first became known to the agency in July of 1933, a year after my birth, my name was given as Howard Green and my mother went by the name Alice Green. Her partner at the time was Howard Green, a friend, whose name I undoubtedly bear. Why else would someone name a child Howard?

When I became fully involved with social services my name was recorded as Howard Green: true name Marshefsky. For whatever reason; it appears that there was a felt need to be deceptive on the part of my mother. Survival must have been extremely difficult and coping may have not been her forte.

It appears that from September 1933 through August of 1935; the burden of our survival as a family became overwhelming. At that time one could not be placed in foster care until they reached the age of three. The state, however, did maintain a list of recommended boarding houses where a parent could, for a small fee, place a child in temporary care.

My mother took advantage of this system for two years. Unfortunately, she found it difficult to pay the fees and I was given the opportunity to travel about the Boston area quite frequently. I lived at various addresses in Malden, Revere, Medford, Somerville and Boston. In all cases I was in residence for one to two months or until the boarding house complained to the state that I was no longer welcome due to non-payment for my care.

In most cases, I taken to each home by my mother but at least on one occasion Howard Green, a family friend, made the placement. Incidentally, my birth mother was using the name of Alice Green at this time.

For a brief period during my second year I lived with my maternal grandmother, Mildred Baxter Foster, and my mother at an address in Boston. Again the posture of a normal family relationship could not be sustained and I was once again relegated to my nomadic life and summarily placed in another boarding house, this time in Medford, when my grandmother agreed to be responsible for my board. Irresponsibility seems to have been a familial trait or perhaps more fairly poverty had taken its toll for I was once again whisked away when the fees went unpaid. This pattern of uncertainty and instability continued over at least a two-year period. I can only piece together the events of this humble beginning through records culled from the archives of the Massachusetts Department of Social Services. I fortunately cannot remember any of these events. I cannot truthfully report any awareness of the obviously unsavory practices of this seriously dysfunctional family dynasty. The patterns of neglect and the possibility of abuse that may have existed in those years obviously impacted on my beginnings. I marvel at the recall of people like; Frank McCort {Angela's Ashes}, who described his sordid years of abject poverty in great detail. At the same time, I am grateful that what I imagine to be a traumatic beginning to my life was forgotten in toto. In addition, I will always be grateful that no kith or kin was available to recount the foibles of a dysfunctional beginning. These two factors are undoubtedly responsible for my chances for forging a future more constructively than one could have predicted.

Hurrah! This chapter comes to a close when at the time I was three years and four months, my birth mother was charged with abandonment of a child in August of 1935. She was found guilty, given probation, and the abandonment charges were dismissed. She defaulted on her probation and absconded. Her whereabouts were not known.

Chapter Two
A New Beginning

At last, I was freed from the bonds of uncertainty. It was August 7th 1935 and I had reached the age where by I could enter into the foster care program provided by the Massachusetts Bureau of Public Welfare. To many, that may not appear to be a reason to rejoice but for me it became an opportunity for stability and the stepping-stone to a better life.

I can't imagine what my thoughts were at the age three but I was accustomed undoubtedly to being shuffled from one "home" to another and learned to adjust to the myriad personalities of adults and other children. I am sure, in most cases, the adults had a difficult time warming up to me, especially when they learned in a short period of time that they would be working on my behalf "pro bono".

After the state completed the appropriate paper work and obligatory physical, I was placed in a temporary home in Dorchester. That scruffy little three-year old must have thought, "Here we go again". Twenty days later I was uprooted and taken to the home of Annie and William Cote who lived in the small rural town of Chelmsford, Massachusetts.

At that juncture of my existence, I am sure that my entire life had been spent in one downtrodden tenement after another in a crowded city environment usually tenanted by strangers. Now I was riding through country roads in a nice car driven by a very personable, friendly lady who really seemed to like me.

The last two sentences are how my imagination has pieced together that new set of events. However, for that three-year old waif, this was where my awareness of life began to evolve. I can remember entering into the kitchen by way of a huge wrap-around porch and standing there with my bag in hand while the caseworker, I believe her name was Mrs. McGrath, and Mrs. Cote chatted pleasantly. I was obviously welcomed although overt over reaction was not a part of Mrs. Cote's character. It was made clear to me by the caseworker, either by word or innuendo that this was to be my new home as long as I was a good boy. This later turned out to be true.

It is hard for me to imagine what this vagabond of three must have thought. The Cotes lived in the country

10

in a single family, seven-room, two-story house. It consisted of three bedrooms upstairs and one down. There was a formal dining room, a living room, a country kitchen with a pantry and a bathroom with the scariest metal, chemical type toilet I had ever seen and there was also a "two-holer" in a back shed.

The house was situated on several acres with a forest on one side and "Clark's Farm" on the other. There was a lot of room to roam. The home was heated with a black iron cook stove in the kitchen, the center of most activities.

When I arrived at the Cote's, there were already three other children in residence. Two were a brother and sister in their late teens and Dickie who was about my age.

Shortly after my arrival, the brother joined the Navy and after a few letters, he faded into his new life, hopefully a rewarding one. His sister remained longer and then struck out on her own. She came back for periodic visits and was always well received. On or about her last visit she came with her boyfriend who was a minor league pitcher. He played catch with me and it was a pleasant visit even though my glove hand ached for a week.

The family now consisted of Dickie and myself as permanent residents, in the best situation that either of us had ever experienced. Since we were not available for adoption, the Cotes became our "parents". I was mommy's boy and Dickie was daddy's boy. There was little competition between us and life was good. We easily adapted to a new way of life. Mrs. Cote became Mama Cote and Mr. Cote became Daddy Billy. Within a short period time, she became Ma and he "Da'billy".

From this point onward all references I make about my mother and father should be considered as a reference to Mrs. or Mr. Cote. We all considered it to be an unconditional fact for the rest of our lives. Much of my writing will be centered on my mother who was always available and the dominant caretaker of the "boys". She was a full time mother and the most accessible parent to us. This is not to diminish the importance of my father whom I greatly admired. He was an influential parental figure but because of his work schedule was not as readily available as my mother.

Perhaps this would be a good juncture to give some insight into the diverse life patterns of each parent. Mr. Cote, "Daddy Billy", grew up in the shoe-manufacturing town of Lawrence, Massachusetts in the late 1800's. He was the youngest of sixteen children and knew the difficulties of poverty. The main fabric of this huge family was his mother whom we called "memere". She was a lovely lady who only spoke Canadian French this was also true of her husband. "Memere" took in washing and ironing and cleaned houses in order to feed the family. Although I never knew her spouse I was led to believe that he rarely worked. The other siblings certainly contributed to the family support as they came of age as did my father who only attended school for six or seven years. He followed the rest of the family into the shoemaking factory and eventually married and had a son. The marriage was short lived and he joined the U S Army Cavalry fought and was wounded in Europe during World War I.

After the war, he ended up in Buffalo, NY where he pitched semi-pro ball for the Niagara Falls team and later became a professional boxer. I always admired his physical strength and his ability to do almost anything with cars and as a wood worker. Upon reflection, he contributed a lot more to my development than I ever realized. Although he rarely attended church he had strong religious convictions and made sure that we attended church and catechism classes. He neither drank, smoked, nor cursed; and I think he saw himself as a "ladies man". He was a good father to us, however, and it never occurred to me to cross him. He and I had a strong bond throughout our lives.

My mother was brought up in Plymouth Union, Vermont. Her parents owned a small farm and a few thousand acres of forestland that included one side of Salt Ash Mountain. They had a maple sugar business and were quite prosperous although they lived the simple life of a small farm family. They grew most of their own food, churned butter, cut wood and carried water from a crystal clear spring-fed brook to the house each day. The mode of carrying the water was a shoulder yoke from which dangled two pails. There was a hand pump on an old soap stone sink in the kitchen and the water was used for cooking and drinking. It was a simple but rewarding life. I accompanied my mother to Vermont on many occasions and have many fond memories of our visits.

My mother graduated from the small country school in Plymouth and received a good education. She read broadly and loved poetry. She married a loyal farm hand that worked on her father's farm. He was ten years older than her and was somewhat abusive and jealous.

She bore a son but the marriage was doomed to failure. Her mother helped her to dissolve the marriage, and sent her to live in Buffalo, NY. Her son remained with his grandmother.

While in Buffalo, she met and married my father. Following the job market they moved to Lowell, Massachusetts in the early thirties

She was a very high-principled woman who never thought poorly of anyone and always encouraged us to do our best. Wherever she went she was always helping and caring for others. In the late thirties and early forties, hobos were a homeless class and never was a vagrant turned away. If one came and asked for water they never left without being fed.

She consistently catered to our needs, guided, and encouraged even the most recalcitrant among us. She contributed more to my development at the emotional, moral and functional level than anyone would normally expect.

She was always the same. I can never remember seeing her angry or overtly pleased. She was always busy but never in a big hurry. Her needlework was outstanding though I often thought my darned socks especially after the third mending were somewhat uncomfortable. Tatting was her forte. When she passed away she left behind a huge box full of her tatting that I foolishly gave away. I had a great deal of difficult dealing with the few possessions she left behind, especially her personal effects.

She had arranged to donate her body for research to the University of Massachusetts Medical School at her death. When her ashes arrived three years later; they remained on a shelf for several more years before her wish to have them scattered in Vermont could be handled. The deed was done, not by my hand. I did drive the car, however, though I never took part in the distribution.

The Buffalo Years – Late 1920's
Mom & Dad Cote
17

Chapter Three

Surviving

When I arrived at my new and final home the records indicate that, with the exception of on-going problems with earaches, my health was good. In a few months this observation would appear to be inaccurate. When I first appeared at the Cote's it was an August day. During the warmer periods of the year my health would invariably improve. As the weather grew colder my health would seriously deteriorate. I would develop a chronic croup and/or bronchitis that would last till late spring. This pattern of various chronic ailments continued until my early teens. Summers would often be a healthy time for me and a relief to the family I am sure.

When you became a ward of the state you were assigned a caseworker. For whatever reason, we always referred to her as the "State Visitor" and she would visit every month. She was always pleasant and encouraging but it was always clear to us that a good report was essential for a stable normal life. She was more like a friend following our progress but if problems presented themselves she was always ready to step in and set the record straight. Though I was never threatened by her visits, I was always embarrassed when she visited at school several times each year. I would be sent to the principal's office and my classmates would wonder what was happening and I would always have an uneasy feeling that I had been discovered.

Within a few years my mother was asked to take more children. She did. Dickie and I now had two more playmates. Needless to say there were some that could not adapt; the one who had the most difficult time was Paul. He was a difficult child to handle. At the end of the kitchen over the pantry door hung a leather strap, a reminder to be good. Paul was often the recipient of its use. He almost seemed to enjoy it and made every attempt to give back as good as he got but my father always won. Paul stayed with us about three years and then was removed.

I never felt the strap nor did anyone else to my recollection. But it always hung on the wall as a vivid reminder of what was possible. Minor infractions led most often to kneeling in the corner until the clock struck "X". I served that sentence on occasion.

Life Starts Anew
as
3Year Olds

Dickie   Howard

Growing older {age five}

Early in life I made a concerted effort to avoid trouble. While others were planning mischief I would generally become involved in solitary play. I had made up my mind not to take the chance of having my parents become disappointed in me. It was a rare event when I dared to break the trust that was becoming part of my character. I was inwardly proud to be known as a "good boy". The state visitor's first report noted that I was a good little boy, clean in habits and obedient. I had a good appetite, could talk plainly, and was very affectionate. She noted that I had a very prominent lower jaw and had a habit of protruding my lower lip. I played well with Dickie and was very quiet. I seemed to be quite at home and could say my name when asked. My mother described me as obedient. It was now October and I had a cold, a pattern that persisted until my early teens.

By Christmas both Dickie and I were solid members of the family. We were seen as normal boys. I enjoyed being waited on, enjoyed attention from others and was lazy. Though my "laziness" persisted for a number of years: it was later that I realized my energy levels were a product of chronic health problems.

21

Three Foster Brothers

Ages five, six, and seven

Howard   Dickie   Paul

Same Crew Three Years Later

Today my situation would be described as Chronic Fatigue Syndrome.

My first Christmas is a vivid memory of an unbelievable array of toys including trucks, a pedal car, clothes and attention galore. I am sure it was an event that I had never experienced. How they ever could afford to shower us in such a lavish manner is beyond my comprehension then and now. They were not wealthy people and only had a few months to prepare, and prepare they did.

The state paid $3.50/month board, a $5 quarterly clothing allowance and all medical bills. They also paid 20 cents for a haircut so my mother learned to cut hair to supplement her income. We always considered barbering her weakest skill. She tended to slide the hand clippers too fast and the result was brutal. We had more hair pulled out by the roots, than was clipped. Luckily, my mother was a very caring person for by January my continuous colds turned into acute bronchitis that I endured for the next ten years as soon as the weather turned a bit cold. The most frequent words spoken by my father were, "Howard, stop your "tussing" {French for coughing}. I am sure it was annoying and I tried to suppress it to no avail.

Maternal Grandparents – Mid 30's – Plymouth Vermont

Family Homestead, Plymouth Vermont
After Hurricane 1938

I was constantly on medication my favorite was Father John's medicine. It tasted really good compared to the doctor's prescriptions. I also became addicted to my mother's home remedy that consisted of a half an un-peeled lemon and a saucer of sugar. I would rub the lemon in the sugar and then suck the lemon juice. It was the most effective medication I took.

I was never allowed outside to play during the winter. The large sunny porch was my outdoor playroom. Nighttime was the worst for all of us as sunset seemed to trigger fits of coughing. My mother never tired of caring for me. I wouldn't have lasted a week in another venue. I was still a good boy in her eyes.

The state visitor was always impressed with my appearance. She noted that I looked healthy but she never visited after sundown. I was always kept clean and on one particular visit, my mother apologized because I was wearing a patched shirt. The caseworker marveled at the amount of clothing I had. Mother accomplished this on the clothing allowance of five dollars every three months and her skill on an old treadle Singer sewing machine augmented by a rich supply of hand-me-downs.

It was now June of 1936. As If my chronic winter maladies were not enough I was now experiencing stomach problems. Acidosis the doctor called it and changes in my diet were recommended. My stomach remained problematic for a number of years, the more reason for mother to pamper me. Not a bad deal! Even though I was now in poor health both winter and summer; I was frequently described as pleasant and a well-behaved boy. I was too sick or weak to be seriously problematic.

My mother would visit her parents in Vermont for several weeks in summer. Only once do I remember my father coming along and on this initial trip, we drove from Chelmsford to Plymouth, Vermont where they lived. On future trips, my mother and I went by train. We boarded the train in Lowell that took us to South Station in Boston, where we changed trains and proceeded to Ludlow, Vermont where her father met us.

Every summer she and I would take this trip together until the late nineteen thirties. Her parents warmed up to me easily as a member of the family. Wow! I now had grandparents. Grandpa involved me in many aspects of farm life. I rode on the hay wagon, walked in the woods, slopped the hogs, was squirted while he milked the cow and cranked the handle of the cream separator. I really liked accompanying him to the brook to fetch water or to watch his pet raccoons walk to the brook on a leash where they would catch fish, and carefully wash them for several minutes and then dine on them. My household chores would include bringing in the firewood and churning cream in a butter churn that looked like a keg on rockers with a stick in the center.

My time in Vermont holds many pleasant memories. Not the least of these was the time my mother, grandmother and I decided to spend some time "up on the hill" that referred to a second farm that was once the homestead and was located on top of Salt Ash Mountain. It was not a high mountain and the abandoned farm was beautiful. It had open hay fields, a small pond loaded with fry, an old cow barn and a house. In those days communication was difficult. No radio or television and telephone service was limited. We were totally unaware that the infamous hurricane of "38" was poised to strike. The second night there we were cognizant of strong winds. We awoke to find the barn roof intact and lying in the meadow and some large trees uprooted. We went to the hill by horse and wagon. When we were ready to go home Reginald, her son, came to tell us it would take a few days to repair the "corduroy bridges" that were washed away before the

27

horses could pass through. He stayed with us for a few days and we had a nice time. We hiked and fished and he told stories of bear and deer much to my enjoyment. The horses finally came and I was allowed to walk down wearing knee high rubber boots that didn't fit and carry a walking stick for help to ford the streams. Back in civilization, we returned to Lowell. It was a grand adventure for a six-year old, but winter was coming, and I was already starting to catch colds as well as dealing with my stomach problems.

I was baptized in St. Mary's Catholic Church in August after we returned from Vermont. Though my father was catholic, my mother was Episcopalian. I don't know how it happened but they were both allowed to be my godparents. Rather ecumenical for those times I think. Baptism didn't have any effect on my health. God must have made the determination that I hadn't suffered enough. At least now I was in a proper state of grace. My mother, a dedicated countrywoman, was very concerned about my eating habits. I only wanted bread and milk to eat. The doctor had decided that my medical condition was more involved then he originally thought. He diagnosed my condition as a highly acid stomach and that I had had rickets at one time, and one side of my body was larger than the other. I also remember that he measured my legs and found one to be longer than the other. He gave my mother some medicine that seemed to be somewhat helpful to my appetite. By December of nineteen thirty-six, my winter health problems were exacerbating. I started off with chicken pox and bronchitis and a bad cold for which I was given a vaccine. Professionals outside the family saw my eating habits as somewhat peculiar. I was very fussy preferring bread and milk of which I drank about two quarts a day and would not eat vegetables or meat. The doctor was not alarmed and said not to worry. My stomach problems were considerable and due to an old "rachitis" condition. I was still everyone's good boy with a pleasant disposition despite all of the health problems. My guess is that I just learned to live with them. Throughout the years when I required constant medical attention most of the doctor's visit were house calls. He was our most frequent visitor. During the winter of nineteen thirty-seven I required a great deal of medical attention. I was treated for constant colds, bronchitis, stomach problems, gripe, both ears were lanced, and a tonsil and adenoid operation performed. Complications occurred a week after the tonsillectomy when my mother discovered I was hemorrhaging and I required a return to the hospital.

By my count during that winter I was hospitalized three times; and house calls by the various doctors numbered between four and ten visits per month. It is interesting to note that the doctors' house calls were less than four dollars per visit. The ear specialist received a total of thirty dollars for his operation and four house calls. The hospital bill for the T&A was seven dollars and the four-day post-op hospital stay was eight dollars and the use of the operating room and anesthesia totaled thirteen dollars. Five home visits after the operation cost twenty-five dollars and ambulance service was one dollar and fifty cents. It is interesting to compare those fee schedules to today's medical costs.

The up side of that winter when I was a burden to the whole community was that I could now swallow food. My appetite improved and I began to eat a broader range of food. After the last operation, the doctor said that I was lucky I didn't choke on the large blood clot in my throat. During or after the operation I also swallowed my tongue. I'm sure that there are a few mean-spirited people who know me well and wish that it would happen again, especially when I forget to allow them to speak during conversations.

Chapter Four

Health and Education

I initially entered the Susan B. McFarlin Elementary School in the fall of 1937. Miss McFarlin lived on our street on a well-kept farm with a huge house, a barn and well-manicured fields. I knew her when she was a retired teacher who lived a somewhat reclusive life. Her father donated the land and helped finance the school bearing her name. She was a pleasant lady who rented stalls in the barn to several people who owned riding horses. When I was older the owners, who never rode their horses, would allow my friends and I to exercise them. I never was a confidant horseman but I did enjoy the experience.

I entered first grade and loved Miss Bridges who was our teacher. By the end of October, I started to miss a great many days because of illness. She saw me as a capable and hard working young man.

By the beginning of November, it became obvious to everyone including the doctor that I should be kept home from school. My mother met with Miss Bridges and agreed to teach me at home. The teacher gave us books and instructions and for most of the school year I was taught at home. Dickie was in the same grade as I. He brought my school lessons back to the teacher as I completed them and often brought homework for me to do.

I would go to visit the teachers periodically and read for them. I also demonstrated my arithmetic skills and they recorded my progress and sanctioned my promotion to the next level.

Though the learning process at home was satisfactory to the school; my memory of the actual learning regimen is very vague. My mother read to me a great deal. Mother Goose and Grimm's Fairy Tales were known by heart. As I continued through the stages of reading we would often go to the library. My doctor's sister was the librarian. As I progressed in reading skills, I can remember reading books such as; Bambi, Little Men, Little Women, and all of Will James' books in the library.

My mother taught me for two hours each day as my health permitted. I also remember doing some drawing and writing exercises using the Palmer method.

I must have done lettering and numbers but my memory is vague about the actual process.

Although my mother was not a teacher she was well educated and dedicated to my progress. I did many things she remembered doing in school and the books I read were often the ones she had read.

The teachers agreed that I was keeping up with the class in the first grade and they were happy with my progress. I probably read more than most of the students in the class. What else was there to do? I was a very slow reader and still am to this day. There were no time restraints. I had all day.

Bronchitis was my biggest nemesis that year. It lasted through August and that was unusual. The good news was that I passed first grade and was allowed to go with my mother to Vermont for a few weeks.

In the second grade I attended school quite regularly. The teacher was well satisfied with my progress but gave me low marks because I rarely finished the assigned tasks. What I did complete was well done and she mistakenly considered me to be very bright.

My lack of appropriate speed was broad based. I was always the last to finish dressing, eating, and performing most any task presented. This weakness in my character presented a problem to most authorities I encountered. They considered me lazy and lacking the relevant energy level required for reasonable progress. It was their responsibility to measure progress and progress required finishing a task.

At home speed was never a requisite. Schoolwork became play and I had all day to finish each assignment. Also, my energy levels at the time were weak and I undoubtedly took advantage of the teaching situation that was largely unstructured.

I would much rather have been considered deeply reflective rather than lazy. The second grade teacher did note that my concentration level was perfect but the thoughts did not manifest themselves on paper.

By the time the cold weather came in November I would no longer be her problem. I dutifully came down with whooping cough and bronchitis and was home schooled again until the first of June. The winter of thirty-nine was difficult, I had every vaccine known to the medical profession. During the month of December the doctor made twelve home visits.

A few days before Christmas, my mother found me crying. She consoled me and eventually found out that because I was so sick and unable to leave the house, I wouldn't be able to see Santa Claus to ask him for a gift for her.

By this time I spent most of the winter in bed. I somehow contracted measles, in addition to my usual maladies. A bed was moved into my mother's room so I could be nursed day and night. Every two hours I was given medication that was brought from Boston. During the measles episode, I had a temperature of 104 degrees and remained delirious for some time. To this day, my sanity is often in question.

The caseworker marveled at the wonderful care, my mother gave me. "As though he was "her own child", she noted. What she didn't realize was that by now I was "her own child".

How much actual schooling I got at home that school year is unknown but it certainly was precious little. However, on June ninth I had entered school for the first full week of classes since the previous November. My mother had taught me through the winter. Undoubtedly with a heavy heart and misty eyes, she saw me promoted to grade three.

Mother and I went to Vermont in July and I came back in good health and remained healthy for the entire summer. The doctor suggested that the time had come to toughen me up and I should be allowed out in all kinds of weather. He felt that I had been babied physically for much too long. He sure knew how to ruin a good thing.

But alas, it seemed to be the best medicine. My appetite improved immeasurably and now ate most everything. The consensus seemed to be that I was extremely well behaved but stubborn as hell. Undoubtedly these terms seem incompatible but everyone appeared to like me. To this day being liked has always been a priority of mine.

I entered the third grade. Everyone was happy with my general persona. The teacher was pleased with my academic progress and behavior. She said I had "good character" and was obedient and dependable. I was also healthier that year and attended school religiously until Thanksgiving. New problems occurred, this time intestinal. The old routine started again. Mother became my teacher again, this time with more structure. My work was sent to school. My mother, justly, got rave reviews from everyone including the school and the state department and many years later from me. She was my full time nurse, teacher of academics, arbiter of proper manners, and my mother.

I think I mirrored her behavior. I was often seen by evaluators as an old fashioned boy. Well mannered, reserved, considerate and an all around good kid. I often wish I could have sustained these characteristics into adulthood.

The usual pattern of poor health seemed to be subsiding somewhat. I attended school through early spring on a regular basis now and began to interact with the other students on the playground with more success.

In the fall of 1940, I was eight plus years of age. My health was much improved. My personal appearance was becoming a problem: shoes untied, shirttails hanging out, and hair uncombed. Mother was not there to attend to my sartorial needs. I was a fourth grader and attended school regularly until the end of December. I was on my own and interacting well with others though my grades were poor and I rarely finished my work. Much too much daydreaming.

By January, my bronchitis returned and remained a problem until April. I got my tutor back. She seemed to relish the task. Now I had plenty of time to do my schoolwork.

I returned to school in April and ended up with average grades for a change. It became obvious that I had missed a lot of the academic basics but I survived.

I put on weight and was described as a big boy for my age though I suspect they were referring to my width. I liked sports, especially baseball. I was never chosen first on "pick up" teams. I was big and slow with no experience. I was a peacemaker. I hated squabbling then and still do even now.

When trouble started I left. Because of my girth, when the most fragile peers were being chased they would cower behind me and beg for protection. I rarely ever interceded physically and the conflict usually ended peacefully.

My favorite sport was boxing, probably because my father had boxed professionally. My father worked nights and my mother would let me listen to the Monday night fights on the radio until long after my eight o'clock bedtime. I was also allowed to listen to the Red Sox on weekends. In those days, the game was all transmitted on ticker tape. You could hear the ticker tape typing in the background and the announcer, I think it was Jim Britt, would read the tape over the air. It would sound something like this "tap-tap-tap- "Ted Willams comes to the plate "tap-tap-tap- "Dizzy Dean throws the ball "tap-tap-tap "inside, ball one" etc.

Summer began and my health improved. My physical stature was described as tall and stocky. I don't know how tall I was but I weighed 140 pounds. Pretty hefty for a nine-year old; no wonder I was slow moving.

The summer was spent primarily outdoors. My mother would frequently pack us a lunch and we would spend the day climbing trees, walking on fallen tree trunks and hiking. Those were peaceful times for us as well as my mother. I often think that she was disappointed when we found our way home.

School started in the fall and I was in the sixth grade. I attended school regularly until February with no major crises. My grades improved. I even got two B's on my report card. That was not to last. I had to take three weeks off for a bout of pan-pharangitis followed by dysentery and a few colds. I was back in school in late March and this time I got three B's and the teacher noted that I could make the first division if I attended school more frequently. She also observed, erroneously, that I resented criticism.

In April, I lost another three weeks with an attack of German measles followed by a second case of measles that brought me to my first bronchial episode that year. The same teacher further besmirched my persona by observing that I craved attention. I could never understand why she couldn't pity me like the others and let me slide. At least, my mother still thought I was wonderful.

Despite a few set backs my physical endurance had improved markedly. In the fall, I entered what is now called junior high school. What it really meant was that I a seventh grader at the McFarlin School.

Chapter Five

A Time of Change

When I entered 7th grade there was sufficient reason to believe that I had academic deficiencies that precluded academic success. My mother deserves a great deal of credit for teaching me under abysmal circumstances. She and she alone took the responsibility for teaching a child who was too involved in surviving from one day to next through a series of devastating illnesses. How she managed to maintain her motivation and at the same time encourage one who was weakened and listless with multiple ailments to read and cipher {her terminology} is certainly remarkable. I was her child and she was not going to let me down. We had developed a closeness that would sustain us throughout our lives.

I was still academically deficient, however. The basic skills and exercises honed by a skilled teacher were not in place. No time constraints were adhered to. The breadth of a full curriculum couldn't be duplicated. Interaction with others, working together and coping with the universal problems one faces culturally were not in my repertoire

On the plus side, I was taught proper behavior and respect. I was made aware of right and wrong as we knew it. When I was young and under her watchful guidance I was considered well behaved and sensitive toward others. As I grew older I still remembered these rules of life though I am not sure that I conformed to them to the degree that I was taught.

Unfortunately the powers in charge made the decision to put me in a slow track grouping. This turned out to be the equivalent of what would be called "a special class" today. Academic work was the slowest most trivial level possible. I did well in this class academics were barely taxing. The deficit remained. The only positive attribute of this experience was that I had the opportunity to develop my social interaction and developed friendships outside the family. There were those who worried about the emerging personality. I was becoming the class clown in a subliminal way. I was careful not to get caught as I was garnering attention. At least I was learning something.

This experience gratefully ended after the first year. The teacher recommended that another student

{my friend} and I move to the 8th grade. One of the
interesting by plays of my seventh grade experience
involved my teacher. She was an old fashioned lady,
strong in character, and rather stern but not mean. She
was also the foster mother of my three sisters.

I was made aware that I had three sisters at an
earlier age. I had never met them and would not for a
number of years. I knew that they lived on a small farm
in West Chelmsford just as I was living on a small farm in
East Chelmsford. I also became aware that my teacher
was their foster parent. I don't know how I knew who she
was but she certainly knew who I was.

For the entire year of her tutelage, there never
once was a hint of our familial ties. It must have been
very difficult for her, but she obviously made the decision
to be a teacher and not a "relative". It put no pressure on
me as her student. She was a teacher and I was a
student and we accepted one another within these
parameters. I was mannerly and she was "teacherly". I
learned later that when I first entered the foster care
program she was approached to consider taking me into
her home. The idea was to try to keep the family
together. She rejected the concept on the grounds that
she knew not how to raise a boy. Three girls were all she

could handle. As it turned out she probably made a good decision. She never could have coped with the constant level of care that was required.

In later years, due to the friendship that developed between my sister, Helen, and me, Mrs. D. and I became better acquainted. Never was the subject of our teacher/student experience ever mentioned. I must admit to being rather humbled by her and always played the role of a well-mannered and friendly fellow.

Helen told me at one time that Mrs. D., probably in a moment of melancholy, told her that she often regretted not keeping us together. She always wanted her girls to go to college. None had. She was very pleased that I went to college. I think I was in graduate school when I last saw her and she was warm and friendly.

It was always Helen's assumption that Mr. D. would have loved to have a boy in the family and would have been a great father. They never had children of their own.

During the summer of 1943, it was decided that it was time to go to work. There were three of us about the same age. I was eleven at the time Dickie and Paul were a bit older. We all wanted bikes and the only way to get them was to earn the money for them.

We got a job on a small farm where the main crop was carrot. We were led to a field that was overgrown with weeds. Closer scrutiny revealed that buried in the weeds were indeed carrots that had never seen sunlight. For ten cents an hour we would crawl along the rows and extract the weeds. Fortunately near the field was a bubbling spring and we would periodically douse our heads with cool water and weed for eight hours.

The farmer was not a pleasant man and was aware that the three of us were state wards. We never saw him when he wasn't angry. On the fourth day we experienced several outbursts of anger. He couldn't find a hoe and raved on about his tools disappearing ever since we began working there. I tried to assure him that we were innocent. He was not appeased and found more reasons for further outbursts.

When we went home I told my mother that I couldn't work there any longer. "Why"? She queried. I explained that the farmer didn't trust us and I didn't want to work for someone who didn't trust me. I waited for a reaction. Instead of being upset she seemed to be proud of my reaction to this bigoted despot. I never went back for my wages though the others continued working on. I became the family farmer to earn my bike.

She had about a half acre of fallow land that had never been farmed or plowed and I spent the summer planting potatoes, corn, and beans in the main garden and lettuce, tomatoes, carrots and beets in the victory garden. I worked all day in the garden until late fall. I enjoyed the work and really earned that bike. By season's end the root cellar was full of carrots and potatoes and my mother was filling the canning cellar.

My father always raised chickens for eggs; when they stopped laying eggs due to their age, they would grace the table in some chicken dish, boiled, roasted or fricasseed. They were so tough that in later life I couldn't think of chicken as an edible dish.

We also had a herd of milking goats; they were in my mother's domain. She did allow me to clean the stalls and carry the grain but they were her pets. The reason for the goats was that the doctor thought goat milk would be good for me. It turned out to be a profitable venture. During the war, my father would sell the milk for 80 cents a quart when we were paying 25 cents for a 2½-gallon pail of cow's milk at the local dairy farm. When my mother became very ill, the goats had to find a new home. I doubt that they were as well cared for again.

In one report to her superiors the state visitor listed my good points as honesty, loyalty, truthfulness, and reticence. Negative qualities included: too easy-going, lacking in initiative and a need to be pushed to accomplishments.

My seventh year of schooling showed a marked improvement in my physical health and school attendance. By the 8th grade all of my ailments seemed to have evaporated. The doctor always felt I would grow out of these afflictions and I did.

My memories of 8th grade from a scholastic point of view are of disaster. I had come to realize that I was gravely deficient in a number of learning skills. Areas such as, grammar, history, geography, and science had never been approached. My confidence level was extremely low. I would sit quietly in my seat praying that I would not be called upon.

In those days you were expected to stand by your seat to answer questions, recite, or read. When called upon, I would nervously rise, certain that my fly was open and attempt to answer. My face would become scarlet and sweat would trickle down my forehead as I stood. When I read I would lose my place and nervously stammer on. When reciting I would forget the words

48

even If I knew them well. I knew everyone was holding back a laugh when I nervously sat down.

I fared better on the playground. I was bigger than most of the others and was almost never challenged. I could hold my own conversing with my male classmates. I could never talk to a girl on purpose and if I had to I would become really flustered. I had to know them well in order not to make a complete fool of myself; I could easily relate to the few girls in my immediate neighborhood but never ventured further.

I was often surprised at how easy it was to mix in with classmates I barely knew. I never remember anyone being uncivil. From the toughest boys in the class to the brightest, from the poorest to the richest, we all interacted harmoniously on the playground.

When I was in the last year of elementary school, I got my first glimpse of my two youngest sisters though we never met.

The high school they attended was at the top of the hill and the McFarlin School was at the bottom. The high school had no lunchroom so the students were allowed to use our facilities.

The students from West Chelmsford attended 7th and 8th grade at the McFarlin School. During recess the high school students passed to the lunchroom. An older friend from West Chelmsford pointed out my sisters to me. On several occasions, we exchanged glances but never met.

Mercifully we all passed into high school. I was not a memorable student during my first year at Chelmsford High. Everyone, myself included, thought it best for me to transfer to Lowell Trade School where I could learn a trade and not be a burden on society.

Several important events occurred in high school that favored my development. Through out my school years my confidence level was seriously impacted. This was undoubtedly fostered by my own interpretation of events and my tendency to worry about how others felt about me. In school I was practically an uncomfortable mute. On the playground and at home I felt comfortable and had normal relationships.

Much of the erosion of confidence I attribute to the high degree of prejudice that was encountered in the immediate environment. Acceptance was varied. Several of our neighbors, with the exception of the farmer next door who hated everyone, saw us as normal kids. As we grew older and were allowed to leave the yard we made some good friends. The adults seemed to be the most wary. There were those who would have preferred we did not exist. One family did not want us to associate with their progeny while others tolerated us.

At school I did not want anyone to know of my home status. As I grew up with my classmates I started to realize that they didn't care who I was or where I came from.

There was a new family in our neighborhood with four boys. The second boy was my age and we hung around together. They were as poor as we were and my friend was rather reckless and a bit wild. Two of the neighbors and I built rafts on Hales Brook near our house. We fished for hornpout and poled our rafts up and down the creek as it wound around the marsh.

One day we went to play on our rafts and found that they had been cut loose. On the way back home we met our new friend. We broached the subject and he replied," Oh! Were they yours?" At that point I lost control and had my first fight. He endured a good thrashing but somehow we remained good friends thereafter.

Later in our relationship a group of us went to a school dance. I managed to hide throughout the event. I knew no one would want to be seen with me and avoided any possibility of making it happen. On the way home there were about five of us walking together and talking when all of a sudden my new neighbor began to berate me for my wall flowerlike behavior. He said he couldn't understand why I wouldn't mix in at the dance. He assured me, in no uncertain terms, that I was as smart and as well dressed and looked as good they did and was well liked by the other kids so what the hell was the matter with me.

After his tirade I felt better about myself. He would never know that his lecture was a turning point in my character development. Metamorphosis was about to take place.

Chapter Six

Adjusting to Change

During the summer of 1945 I met my sister, Helen. I was working in the garden when a car drove up with two strangers in the front seat. It was my sister and her fiancé. We talked and went for a ride. They had set their wedding date and wanted me to attend. That was the start of a life long friendship. I was very shy and lacking in social confidence and did not much relish the idea of spending the whole day with a group of people I never saw before.

I went to their wedding and although I was uncomfortable socially everyone was pleasant and attempted to engage me in conversation. I tried though I don't think I was successful.

It was at the same gathering that I met my other two sisters. I don't remember having a conversation with them but I am sure we were introduced and exchanged a few uncomfortable moments. Neither my other sisters nor I ever developed a sustaining relationship. We each went down different pathways in our lives and rarely saw one another or had the genuine inclination to build a kinship.

Helen and her husband, Ralph, who recently passed away and our families are friends as well as an extended family today.

An interesting side note developed about ten years later. When I entered Fitchburg State College in 1954 one of the other students had the same last name as one of my sisters. He was my brother-in-law.

For me, high school {ninth grade} was a non-event. I attended regularly but was simply not ready for the rigor of academics. I sat in my seat and tried to look studious and interested though in some classes I barely knew what the teachers were talking about. I was in the lowest academic track and couldn't keep up. No one gave me any grief and I reciprocated in kind. I enjoyed the atmosphere. I went to all of the football and basketball games and was encouraged to join the football team the following year.

Though my health was good in 9th grade I developed a new problem that certainly didn't help my confidence or demeanor. This new dilemma came as what the doctor called furunculosis {neck boils}. They were painful and ugly and had to be lanced and drained periodically which was not pleasant. In addition the medication of choice was a salve called ergophine. It looked like tar and stained your collar yellow despite the bandages. This was not a confidence builder for a young man entering puberty.

I was obviously not going to be a scholar. My grades were mostly D's with an occasional C or even a rare B in an easy subject. I was discouraged. The state visitor and I discussed entering trade school in Lowell. The idea appealed to me. They did not want me to become a burden on society nor did I want to be. I was starting to become more ambitious and hadn't heard the word lazy for some time. I was growing out of the plethora of maladies discussed in previous chapters just as the doctors predicted. I was considered strong and healthy and relished manual labor, especially on payday.

In the summer over the years, we would pick blueberries and sell them going door to door for 15 cents a quart. I was the family gardener. I had a paper route and rode my bike for about 10 miles each day, rain or shine.

A neighbor bought a house without a cellar, and I spent two summers digging out the cellar and hauling out pails of sand. When I finished a section the mason would come and build a wall with blocks. The two women who lived there were very friendly and treated me well for a number of years. I continued to work on carpentry projects for them until I graduated from trade school.

My mother became ill during the summer of 1946. At this point in time I was the only foster child of the original four that remained at home. One child was in reform school; he had a variety of problems including what my father referred to as "long fingers". Setting fires in the woods near our house was his downfall. The fire department became suspicious of him when he was always there to help put out the fires.

There were several new members of the family who came later with no significant problems and remained through high school. We all got along well and I was the big brother. If someone erred and I was near I would always be to blame for not stopping the infraction. I was bigger and should know better.

My role in the family increased when my mother was operated upon. Her diagnosis was a strangulated intestine that was resected along with a portion of her stomach. I was large and in charge! I cooked, cleaned, nursed and watched over the family. The garden was much smaller that year. We all survived. It felt good to reciprocate after all those years of being the recipient. We were a solid family. Three years later I was to get another chance to help.

Trade school was my choice. I took the initiative and registered on my own with the support of the family and the state. In those days trade school was a dumping ground. We were certainly a bunch of misfits. Three quarters of the class intended to quit school and most lived up to that expectation when they reached 16. I think that there were about ten of us left at graduation time in 1949. It was a pretty rough group that had not achieved academically before entering. Academics were not our forte and were the weakest part of the curriculum. Book learning was virtually non-existent.

The schedule was much as it is today, one week in shop and one week of academics. Everyone attended shop but attendance was poor during academic week. I adjusted well and really enjoyed going to school for the first time in my life. I was a straight A student for three years. At graduation I was the valedictorian.

The unfortunate deficiency of the program was the academics. Trade school students were not expected to go on to college. We were to enter the various trades.

We were taught the rudiments of our chosen trade and practiced the various skills that were needed.

In March of 1949, the year of graduation, my father took ill. His diagnosis was a blood clot on the right hemisphere of the brain. He went into a coma. The doctors did what they could but brain surgery was not an option at the time.

He was in a coma for nearly a month when one of the doctors heard of an experimental procedure in brain surgery being done at Cushing Veterans Hospital in Natick, Massachusetts. My mother contacted the Veterans Administration and they acted quickly. Two days later while still in a coma he was rushed to Cushing by ambulance. He was operated on the next day under local anesthesia. They removed bone in the area of the clot to extract it. He was immediately conscious and the doctor asked him if he remembered his army serial number. He rattled it off and added, "No one ever forgets his serial number, you stupid S.O.B.". In time he made a full recovery.

During the three years I attended trade school we lived in Chelmsford. The school was in Lowell where my father was manager of an office building. He kept the building and offices clean, tended the boiler, and ran the elevator. He had one assistant. The building was within four blocks of the school so I accompanied him to work each morning and then walked to school. When classes were over I would return and help run the elevator until he left at 5 PM.

When he was taken ill the owner of the building allowed me to continue in his absence and adjusted the hours to accommodate the other employee.

My routine changed for the next four months. I got up at 4AM, had breakfast and walked two miles to catch the bus to Lowell. I swept the floor, emptied wastebaskets, polished the brass fixtures occasionally, and then left for school. After school I returned and ran the elevator until 9 PM, rode the bus and then walked the last two miles home. My mother would be waiting with a snack and we would talk. It turned out that my father was a poor money manager. We were in serious debt but by the time he returned to work, we had repaid his debts and were again solvent.

Chapter Seven

Work and Opportunity

At last I graduated from Lowell Trade School. My health was fine and had been for the last three years. You will read no more about my abysmal health until I reach my mid-fifties.

I turned seventeen in April of the year I graduated. I wasn't old enough to join the carpenter's union as an apprentice and the small builders were fully staffed.

A friend got me a job with a big potato farmer in Concord. It was hard work. I really enjoyed farming but by late fall the potatoes would be harvested, graded, bagged and marketed; the job was temporary.

As late fall approached I was offered a job pasteurizing and bottling milk at a small dairy. It was a one - man operation and very close to our house. The down side was that the work started at 5AM. The owner was a good friend. He showed me the routine for a week and then I was on my own. I liked the job. I was home by 1 or 2 PM and could pick up an occasional job around the neighborhood doing building repairs.

At this same time I got my first car, a 1933 Chevy sedan. I was maturing fast and from my mother's point of view much too fast. She was not aware that I stayed pretty much within the behavioral patterns that she had set for me early in life. What she knew was that I was out almost nightly and was never in bed by 9 as had been our standard ritual. She could be imaginative and feared the worst.

I traveled with friends that were older than I was. She had no reason to worry though later experience taught me that that is what mothers do.

I enjoyed dancing and spent at least one night a week pursuing this pleasure. There were several ballrooms in and around the area and my friends and I were regular patrons. No drinking was allowed and the music was to our liking.

Later on I got interested in Jazz. Lowell was in the loop and a lot of the great jazz musicians would pass through town and play at the various clubs. Groups of us would go to these concerts and I was always the designated driver. I was intrigued by the fact that I had as much or more fun at these events and could tell them the next day how much fun they had had the previous evening.

At the end of May 1950, my old principal from trade school called me at home and asked me if I would come to his office. I visited him the next day and received a warm welcome. We talked for a while and the conversation lead to my hopes for the future. I told him that I was happy at my job and that I intended to go into the carpentry apprentice program in the near future.

He asked how I felt about going to college and becoming a teacher. I was stunned and told him that I had never considered it. He asked why. I told him that I felt that I was not able to handle college academic courses and that I couldn't possibly imagine having enough money to go at any time in the near future even if I could somehow prepare for the academic program. He indicated that there might be ways to get tuition waivers and that he would talk to the state about extending their financial support.

He continued to encourage me. No one from his school had ever gone to college and I was his chosen candidate. I was flustered but flattered. I gave the idea a lot of thought and began to wonder if I could actually pull it off. During the summer I day dreamed about the possibility but made little progress toward saving the money needed. To me it was an astronomical undertaking. My academic skills had not been enhanced that summer and I knew I needed to become better prepared before I could realistically consider pursuing a college program.

The important reality that was fostered that summer was the introduction and subsequent realization that there was a way of life possible that I had never even considered.

My mind had been jogged. The prospects for making a living in Lowell were always a bit troubling in my mind. Carpentry was my preference but the prospect of winter layoffs and limited demand for workers always bothered me. The other prospect was laboring in the woolen mills that interested me not even a little.

My mindset was now oriented to further schooling. The difficulty now was how to execute this ideal. The answer to this bifurcated question became obvious.

The Korean War was in full progress. Uncle Sam needed my help. The chances were about one hundred percent certain that if I didn't enlist I would soon be drafted. By enlisting I could resolve two problems. I would have four years to develop more reasonable academic skills and I would be eligible for the GI Bill.

I chose the Air Force. The chance to obtain further education was almost a certainty. Everyone who was accepted was sent to a school after completing basic training. I took the required test. The recruiters were amazed. My score was nearly perfect, {they neglected to tell me that nearly everyone scored at the genius level}.

"Sign here". I did.

Chapter Eight

Maturity Accelerates

I now made the biggest decision of my life. With the exception of occasional trips to Vermont with my mother I had never ventured beyond a twenty-five mile radius from my home in Chelmsford.

The resolve to enlist in the air force for a term of four years at first appeared to be excessively long. The benefits I was to receive, however, were greater than I had hoped for. In addition to schooling and the ability to travel about the country at government expense, the experience was a positive one. I grew more confident and self-assured though of late I had made progress in that direction. The next four years would add the finishing touches that were sorely needed.

Through the years my father and I had formed a bond that I had never quite recognized. When I was young mother was the dominant figure in the household. As our immediate family began to grow he would often take us to various lakes to swim and bathe which was a popular custom in those days. Ice cream treats on a hot summer evening were also common. When I was in my teens he and I would also attend the auto races nearly every week at the Dracut Speedway.

He was strong physically and in many ways had a tough veneer. He belonged to the Police Auxiliary in Lowell but I never quite knew what his role was. He was not one to cross.

His enjoyments were basic. When the circus came to town we would arise at 4 AM and watch them unload the trains and then parade to the fairgrounds where they would set up the big top using the elephants to raise the huge tent.

He was religious though he rarely attended church. Once when we were following a funeral procession, an impatient driver passed the slow moving caravan. My father raced after him, pulled him over and rather loudly and physically explained to the startled stranger that he had erred.

On the appointed day he drove me to the induction center. When I got out we shook hands. No words were exchanged. The tears running down his cheeks said it all.

There were about twenty of us inducted that day. We swore an oath of allegiance to God and country and

66

were then ordered into a room for a medical examination. We stood side by side and were ordered to drop our drawers. We glanced at one another uncomfortably and obeyed. The doctor entered. In order we said, "ahs", coughed and pulled up our pants. No one failed.

We boarded a bus to Boston where we met the rest of our contingent and left by train for San Antonio, Texas for basic training. One of the somewhat older members of our group, an ex–merchant marine, was appointed as our group leader. We changed trains in St Louis. There was a mix up; our train was over crowded and all seats were taken. Luckily our leader was up to the challenge. We all had first class tickets and a planned itinerary. The end result was he negotiated an upgrade for ten two – man private staterooms. We rode in splendor. Each room had two bunks, a sofa, a chair, wash basin and toilet. The last three amenities were a brilliantly designed single piece.

That afternoon we met up with a group from Tennessee. They talked kind of strangely but seemed to be nice guys. We went to supper together. Our waiter was a young fast-talking black man. He talked incessantly as he brought our water glasses and with a professional flair poured the water. When he was finished the Tennessean opposite me cleared the table of all its contents with one fell swoop of his arm, breaking glasses and splashing water flew everywhere. We protested. He responded, "Didn't you see what that "nigger" did, he put his fingers in our glasses". The headwaiter came over and asked what happened. After our comrade explained the seasoned waiter nodded and said, "I understand I will be your waiter now." The trouble was over and I had witnessed for the first time, racial prejudice.

The rest of the trip was enjoyable. The enlistees from Massachusetts enjoyed the luxury accommodations though we spent most of the time in the Pullman car with the boys from Tennessee.

On the second day we arrived in Texas and boarded a train for Shepard Air Force Base in San Antonio. The train was right out of the television program, "Petticoat Junction", complete with clouds of black smoke puffing from its stack. We arrived in a rainstorm and marched to our barracks in a sea of mud. The next day we were marched to the quartermaster and received our new wardrobe and the obligatory GI haircut. We looked like prisoners and for the next eight weeks we were. Our civilian clothes were mailed home. My mother kept my mud -encrusted shoes for many years, a precious souvenir.

Those first eight weeks were difficult on us all but to a few they were devastating. A handful of those beleaguered souls were given an incompatibility discharge. To me it was a great adventure though I was not immune to becoming homesick.

We would sit on our cots and exchange stories. I thought that the speech of those from the South and West really sounded odd. One evening I was asked to join a group that spoke with heavy regional accents. I was asked to say, "I parked the car in Harvard Yard." In a clear Boston accent I did as they bid. They roared with laughter. They offered further tests and again roared at my accent. I didn't get the point. I thought I sounded great compared to them. The teasing went on for several days. In an effort to extricate myself from this harassment I finally asked if I could pose a question. They consented. With all the seriousness I could muster I asked, "Why do you all hate Negroes so intensely and yet adopt their accent when speaking?" My own regional inflection became a non-issue.

In our unit we had only one black person. I had never spoken to one before. I was a bit uncomfortable around him and I imagine he sensed it. One evening I was to relieve him on guard duty. He approached me and offered the observation that when I was to relieve him it would be dark and he would be hard to find under those conditions. That broke the tension and we became good friends.

Near the end of basic training we took placement tests prior to our next assignment. I scored high in three categories; air traffic control, clerk typist, and airplane mechanic. The air force obviously needed mechanics and shipped me to Wichita Falls, Texas for aircraft and engine maintenance, an eight-month program. It would not have been my choice though I was encouraged by the positive reactions of those in my unit. The school certainly exceeded my expectations. It was a rigorous and well-organized education with a written test at the end of each segment. I not only got a good education during those eight months but I was also growing up fast. Upon graduation we were all awarded an M.O.S 43-121 that was the entry-level skill level for mechanics. I was sent to Scott Air Force Base in Belleville, Illinois where I became the crew chief on a C-45 in the base flight squadron. Once out of school, there was a lot more freedom then in any of the other branches of service.

Private Marchie –1950 –San Antonio

Friends – Scott Air Force Base - 1951

71

No more roll call or drill sergeants, very little marching and spit and polish hardly existed. The barrack was clean and tidy and inspections were reasonable. Everyone had an assignment and was expected to fulfil the obligation.

I had been away from home for nearly a year. My original goals remained. I talked to a lot of people. Intellectually, I still felt inadequate to many of my associates. I wanted to know what they knew. I started to read Time magazine to try to develop an awareness of politics, world events, the arts and anything I felt weak in.

In the evenings we would often sit on our bunks and talk about what we would do after we were discharged. There was a radioman in our barracks by the name of Jimmy Banks. He had entered the service in order to qualify for the GI Bill so that he could finish his PHD in Arts at Washington University in St Louis. Up to this time he was the brightest person that I had encountered. He was a master of language; there was no word in the dictionary that he could not define. There was no piece of music or work of art that he was unfamiliar to him. He was black, cultured and a very good friend.

72

I had never been to a museum; so we went. He put together a list of books that I should be familiar with. I read Poe, Sinclair Lewis, Dickens, and Shakespeare whom I didn't understand. I was catching up and my comfort level began to increase. I read books on art and the librettos of operas.

I could communicate my thoughts adequately though vocabulary was not a strong point. I had never given language development much thought and I discovered that one could analyze word meanings by simply acquiring knowledge of Latin and Greek roots. This was an intriguing discovery essential to the growth of my vocabulary. I must admit to not becoming an egghead. There were, however, sufficient opportunities to become involved in a variety of life broadening activities that raised social awareness; and I took what I could from these experiences.

I really enjoyed the St Louis area. There were the Jazz clubs, dance parties on the Mississippi River Boat, the Admiral, and pleasant trips to Forest Park and the surrounding countryside. Pure culture shock for the small town overprotected boy.

All good things come to an end I learned. The Air Force decided that more travel was needed to broaden my experience. I was sent to Korea.

Chapter Nine

The Korean Era

Before going to Korea, as was the custom of the government, I was granted a month's leave as well as money for travel by rail and a month's pay. Since I was on flying status an additional thirty-five dollars was included. With one hundred thirty-five dollars and a train ticket, I traveled home, stayed three weeks and then traveled across country to San Francisco and I still had money in my pocket.

We were processed at an old army base in Pittsburg, CA. I was assigned number two thousand two hundred and sixty-eight. Each day I would get in line with two thousand two hundred and sixty seven people before me for medical checks, shots, record processing and payroll status data. The lines were long and moved slowly. Finally the long wait was over. We were transported to dockside and again stood in a line that barely moved. The ship was the biggest I had ever seen it was about ten stories high and a half-mile long I thought. I was the twentieth man from the gangplank when the line stopped. The ship was full. We were carted back to Pittburg to await the next ship. We were not told that we were alternates.

Several days later we got orders to move out again. I was now number twenty-eight and a member of the "advance party". We even rated our own bus. Spirits rose. This was quite an honor. Our smug group boarded first. We were assigned quarters in the bow of the ship. Wow! We chose bunks and settled in. We were ordered to report on deck for inspection.

The inspection was weird, no saying "ah" or coughing with our pants down. Instead the emphasis was on cleanliness our fingernails were examined. It was at this time that we learned the essence of being the "advance party". For the next twenty-eight days we were on K.P. They were twenty-eight of the sickest days that I had ever endured. The only thing that made me grateful was the realization of how lucky I was not to have enlisted in the Navy.

Yet, even this experience was broadening. I had traveled cross-country by train and now was on a huge transport ship on the Pacific Ocean about to cross the International Date Line. I had never heard of this feature of our world nor was I acquainted with the Order of King Neptune in which I was now a bona fide member.

By the time our ship anchored in Yokohama, Japan I had lost twelve pounds. These were exciting times. Within the next two weeks I was to travel across two foreign countries.

We disembarked on the next day and boarded a troop train for our next destination, Iwakuni. The rail trip across Japan was fascinating and about four hundred miles long. The troop train was much like any coach car except for the toilet facility that consisted of a small empty room with a six inch by thirty-six inch slot in the floor. In front of the slot sat a twelve-inch brass pole horizontal to the floor and about six inches high. One would straddle the slot and grasp the pole to relieve oneself. From there the waste would fall to the track. It was a bit unconventional but worked well.

It seemed like every village, waterway, field, and the general landscape was an artist's dream. The homes in the villages had thatched roofs and the people appeared just as I had imagined. The train followed a route through cities that I would read about many years later. Some of the industrial areas, especially Hiroshima, still showed scars from World War Two.

Troop Train from Tokyo to Iwakuni

Hiroshima 1952

Village

We were billeted in a huge complex in Iwakuni. There was a center court the size of a football field. We fell out every morning for roll call and were given orders for the day. We were there for only a few days awaiting transportation to our post in Korea. We were allowed to go into town one day. The main road was of dirt and lined with picturesque thatched roof shops and houses. It was right out of a movie set. The people were busy but pleasant they wore the most beautiful, classic clothing imaginable. The unfamiliar feel of dampness and the odor of exotic foods were somewhat disconcerting but only made the experience more authentic. It fostered a deep interest in their art as well as the culture that remains to this day.

The plane finally arrived to whisk a small group of us to the town of Pyong-Taec, Korea where we would be stationed for six months. Our outfit, the 3847 Tack Control Group, would then move forward to the end of the railhead at the city of ChinChon.

Our aircraft consisted of a small fleet of C-47 cargo planes loaded with radio equipment. It was actually a flying radio transmission station. There was also a much larger fleet of T-6's. The T-6 was a pilot training plane in the States.

Labor Intensive Building Construction – Pyong-Taek

In Korea it was armed with white phosphorous rockets that were used to mark enemy positions identified by the army. We would find the targeted gun position and release the rockets that after contact would emit a cloud of smoke. The position would then be radioed through the relay station to the jets that would then attempt to destroy the enemy position.

The T-6 was a two-man tandem plane that could fly low and slowly giving the observer more opportunity to find the offending target. Getting back to the base could become a little hairy as the enemy would take umbrage at being interrupted in their effort to advance their unit and would now have to endure a thorough bombing attack on their position.

Each crew chief had a plane to keep in repair. I can only remember one of our planes being shot down. They would often be shot up quite badly but would be repaired and back in action quickly.

Although we were the closest air base to the front lines we never experienced a single air raid. A small plane similar to a single engine piper cub known as "Bed Check Charlie" would occasionally drop leaflets on our base but they didn't hurt much.

Most days we could hear the distant rumble of artillery exchanges. We were only a few miles from a MASH Unit. During bad weather, not infrequent, military helicopters would land at our base and ambulances would rush wounded to the MASH facility. This was a grim reminder to those of us who only experienced the war repairing the damage inflicted upon our planes by the enemy.

For a year we lived in a twelve-man tent that had a wooden floor and was warmed by an oil space heater. Each tent was assigned a Korean "house-boy" who was practically adopted and considered family. Kim, our houseboy, was well treated. In the winter he would sleep in the tent rather than in the quarters designated for houseboys. He was well fed and learned English quickly. He would look through our magazines and gaze in awe at the houses, cars, and clothes that we took for granted. It was every houseboy's dream that one of us would send for him upon our return to the States.

Our tent, with one exception, was comprised of a congenial close-knit group. We drank {3.2 beer} together and exchanged news, letters, and packages from home. We played pranks on each other and generally enjoyed our time off together.

82

Government Quarters – Chunchon - 1952

Party Time

Tent City – K – 38, 1952

My friend from St Louis lived a few tents away and spent a lot of time with us. He continued to urge me to read. We checked out the company's sparse selection of books and I proceeded to get "caught up" with my peers. I still received "Time Magazine" which I read from cover to cover.

Most of those in our tent were older more mature men who had been in the National Guard when their unit was activated. They had growing families back home and for the most part were very stable people who were not opposed to raising a little hell. I helped the best I could.

I was interviewed for promotion to corporal. A master sergeant asked me where the thermocouple was located in the C-47. I told him that the tech orders designate cylinder X but our planes all had been changed to cylinder Y to prevent a false over heating reading in the cockpit. He assured the group I was wrong. He also asked me who Mendoza Francais was. I told him I wasn't familiar with him. He assured me that I knew him as the President of France. "Oh, you mean Mendes France" I replied and continued to elaborate on what I knew. I was sure I had blown it badly.

Rail and Pedestrian Transportation in Korea, 1952

Scenes City of Chunchon 1952

T-6 Flight Line   Chunchon, Korea

Barely made it Home   Glad to be Back

I not only got my stripe but I had my MOS up graded to a 43151, a full-fledged mechanic.

Briefly after my promotion a group of us were being transported in an open "four-by" army truck to a work detail. As we drove we would pass lines of women walking along the roadside drainage ditches with all their belongings on their backs and in bundles on their heads. One of the GI's was amusing himself and others by poking the parcels on their heads with a pole knocking the unfortunate defenseless women into the drainage ditch. I interceded. I took the pole and threw it out of the truck. In the ensuing scuffle he became indignant and reacted. I was singled out as the culprit and had to report to the unit's captain to explain. I did. He dismissed the witnesses, closed the door, shook my hand and thanked me.

I always disliked Ike {Eisenhower}. I thought Adlai Stevenson was the better choice. Ike campaigned on the promise that he would go to Korea and he did causing my R&R {rest and relaxation} trip to Tokyo to be cancelled. . He never apologized. I never forgave him. I did go two weeks later and had a fabulous time.

R and R consisted of a five day "vacation" in Tokyo, Japan. We flew into an Air Force Base near

Tokyo and hired a taxi to take us into the city. The cabdriver preferred to use the horn rather than the brakes. This made for a hair-raising ride. We felt safer in Korea.

Since we knew not where to go the cabdriver chose our destination a small attractive hotel outside of downtown. We paid with "script" {U.S. Government-issue paper money} and he happily drove off.

After registering us the owner paraded a bevy of companions for us to choose from. They were very pleasant and treated us well. The bathing system was much like today's use of the hot tub. First one showered and then soaked. It was a new experience for me however.

My companion turned out to be a worthy travel guide. I saw the city through the eyes of a native. We visited the seaside where she introduced me to dried squid. She relished hers and mine. We also wandered about the Ginza shopping at the huge department stores. The boutiques, dance halls and the amusement arcade were also unique.

We fed the koi {fish} in the moat surrounding the Emperors' Palace. The Shinto Shrines standing in the small neat parks about the city fascinated me. The mode

90

of dress, the architecture of the buildings, and the hustle and bustle of the people going about on their routines were sensually appealing.

Even getting a haircut was an experience to remember. First a haircut and a shave followed by a mudpack facial next came a relaxing shoulder and neck massage and all for a quarter.

I spent the last two days staying at The Airmen's Club in the New Carjon {my spelling} building where I had my first real dinners outside a mess hall in nearly a year while listening to an all-Japanese jazz band.

The mores of Japan and Korea were far different than those in America. It was easy to become wantonly excessive. Most Americans behaved honorably and profited from the experience while others overreacted to the relaxed mores.

The flight back to duty in Korea was uneventful except for one last look at the snowcapped peak of Mt. Fujiyama.

In January of 1953 I returned to the States. The trip was more pleasant this time. No KP and I weathered several vicious storms without seasickness while waves broke over the bow of the huge ship that was at least 10 stories high.

Sailing to Japan

East meets West

Tokyo

School Girls

Imperial Palace, Tokyo, Japan 1952

Main Gate

Guards' Quarters

Imperial Coach

When I left San Francisco the previous year it was raining. As we sailed under the Golden Gate Bridge it was still raining.

We docked and disembarked on Treasure Island with no fanfare. It was another non-event. After all, our government had never declared war it was merely a police action. Not a good explanation for the countless thousands of families that lost husbands, fathers, sons and friends.

The "Korean Conflict" is seriously misunderstood today. One had to live in those precarious times to truly understand. The Russian communists had already absorbed many countries in Europe. The Chinese communists were doing the same in Asia with frightening success. World domination was their avowed ultimate goal. It was hard to deny the progress already achieved. Communist missiles were specifically aimed at the United States and the technology to exercise a strike was fast approaching. They already had voiced their commitment to destroy us.

Korea was our government's attempt to contain Communism in Asia and to a degree we were successful. Then, just as in the Viet Nam conflict, there were varying points of view but the opposition lacked the organizational skills that were evident in the latter controversy.

The outcome was the same, however. We came home thinking that we had stemmed the tide of proliferation but to the naysayers we were killers. It took thirty more years before communism self-destructed in Europe but it didn't happen unilaterally. Recent examples in China send mixed messages verifying that they are not yet out of the woods. I still feel that what we did was not in vain and in fact speeded the effort toward the demise of the world dominance ideal. I also feel the government should proceed carefully with communist nations. Their ideals are improving but we should exercise caution until they fully evolve in a variety of areas. I never regretted my assignment in Korea. Attitudes were different in the fifties and I would have been disappointed if I had missed that opportunity. It was another step in the process of evolving into manhood.

I finished my tour of duty in Korea and after a month's leave assumed my new duties at Vance Air Force Base in Enid, OK.

Chapter Ten

A New Direction

Before coming home from Korea I had established the practice of sending money to my father each month. The goal was to have transportation {a car} while on leave. I wrote and asked him to buy a car for me before I arrived home. Mom wrote back asking how much money I had sent. I told her it totaled $1200. We were shocked to find out that he had spent all but two hundred. Managing money was not his strength.

When I finally arrived home in the driveway sat a beautiful Buick Roadmaster, obviously meant to be chauffeur driven. I was stunned! He had put a few hundred dollars down and earned himself a reprieve. It was a great car with a Dynaflow transmission and would pass anything on the road but a gas station.

Within a few weeks I was on my way to Vance Air Force Base in Enid. I decided to go by train and left the car at home. My dad drove it for a while and eventually sold it. I was leery of driving the car back to the base. There were no super highways then which made cross-country driving a long slow process. I was sure I would get lost in mid America somewhere, or have a mechanical problem or an accident. The easiest way out was to go by train.

I got to Oklahoma and started the last phase of my military career. I really liked the area. The people were the main asset both on base and off. The countryside was generally flat and extensively farmed. In the northwest the terrain was more interesting with a few small mountains. Oil fields were everywhere, even on the lawn of the state capitol building in Oklahoma City. Overall it was a pleasant place to be with one exception, the weather. The summers were hot and muggy. There was little snow in winter and the temperature was more moderate than that of New England. The winds were bone chilling in winter and in summer felt like a blast furnace. The area was subject to tornadoes and dust storms and these were often a concern on the flight line.

I was assigned to base flight that was responsible for the airplanes used by the military administrators. I became the crew chief of a C-47 cargo plane. My obligation was to perform all necessary maintenance on the aircraft and to fly with it wherever it went.

Every morning the plane was carefully inspected cleaned and maintained according to a standard checklist. It would then be taxied to a determined area to power check the engine, test the brakes, ailerons, rudder, flaps, and all moveable parts necessary to operate the craft as well as the radio.

I got to see a lot more of the country at government expense. Life was good, both socially and in the workplace. During my tenure at Vance I also crewed a C-45 and a B-25. The C-45 was often put to use by the base commander and his staff. It was a small passenger plane with room for six to eight passengers. It was a great little plane with one basic flaw. The entrance door would sometimes come ajar during flight. It was not a serious problem as the outside pressure on the door prevented opening, hence it would usually go undetected except for a soft hissing sound. The assistant base commander was a particularly cantankerous colonel. One day he noticed the problem and placed the plane on red X that meant the plane was grounded until repaired. It was my responsibility to make the repair. Knowing his reputation I took no chances. I removed the offending door, took it to the base shop then installed a new door and signed it off.

Pre-Flighting - C-45 Oklahoma-1953

Several days later he returned to fly the plane. He checked the form and noted that I had made the repair. He boarded the plane, closed the door tightly and then rammed the door with his shoulder. The door popped open and he promptly rolled onto the tarmac. He wasn't too damned pleased. He stormed off to raise some hell. I was in the clear. His argument was with the base shop. They apparently were better able to explain the problem than I was. He returned and took the plane out. The door remained latched.

I wasn't as lucky about six months later. I was crewing on a B-25 by that time. I had checked out the plane and determined that it needed a new starter. I removed the starter leaving the cowling on the engine. A new starter was procured at the base shop. While I was gone another crew chief on the line in front of my plane power checked his engine causing the cowling to blow off into the windshield causing it to shatter. It was against rules to power check an engine on line but guess who was in trouble. It was I, the guy who didn't secure the cowling. The sergeant's pet just made an honest mistake.

A few days later a pilot requested that I be his chief on a flight. He checked out the assigned plane and he was dissatisfied and requested another. It was deemed OK. He made the necessary changes at base flight but in the process the "Form 1" was left on the counter and we took off. That was not good. The form is always kept in the aircraft as it contains the maintenance history and any idiosyncrasies.

We took off and headed for Ogden, UT, our destination. While crossing the Rockies we passed through a cloud rising from the valley floor. When we emerged from this cloud the voltage regulators were smoking badly. I removed both of the offending regulators and threw them out the co-pilot's window. We were now without electricity. The pilots had been flying by radio compass and had no idea where we were. I was more concerned about my burnt hands. Finding the way was their responsibility but one look at the gas gauge convinced me I should help. I had always wanted to experience a parachute jump but now had second thoughts. We poured over maps and finally the co-pilot spotted a tower-like structure. It was located on the map and the flight to Ogden was now a given. We flew over the base rocking our wings indicating to the tower that this was an emergency. The fire trucks came and proceeded to spread foam on the runway. I manually cranked down the landing gear but could not determine if the locking mechanism was deployed. Fortunately it was. We landed feeling pretty good about ourselves only to discover the "Form 1" was not on board. I procured a new form and red Xed the plane.

We remained there for several days since they had no B-25 parts on base. The regulators had to be flown in. I slept on board. The new parts arrived, the plane checked out fine and we returned to Vance. We were well received by the other crews until I met the sergeant who was all smiles as he held the original form in his hand. He took me into his office and gave me a proper dressing down. He ranted on for some time and then went to lunch. The others gathered around and asked me how it went. I spotted his empty desk and jumped atop it and began jumping up and down repeating the sergeant's unkind words about my competence and my lack of innate intelligence. During my impromptu performance I bent over and pounded my fists on the desk while berating myself. I looked up and saw the sergeant watching my performance through the window in the door. He proceeded to the captain's office to initiate a court martial.

The captain called me in and asked me to explain. I did and he laughed until the tears ran down his cheeks. He told me not to worry as long as I kept my mouth shut about his reaction. He told the sergeant that because I was the only Korean War veteran in his outfit he would not proceed further. I became a folk hero for a time and never erred again.

As I previously noted I really liked Oklahoma. I liked the duty, enjoyed the people and they seemed to feel the same. For the first time in my life I had a steady girl friend and a solid social life. I belonged to the Deleron Club and eventually bought a car with the help of my girl friend. Actually she was a woman quite a few years older than I. We were very compatible and spent most of our spare time together. She was interested in making a life together but the age difference and the idea of never leaving Oklahoma brought me to my senses eventually.

Enid was in a dry county so in order to partake of alcohol you had to belong to a social club run by the local bootleggers. Juice cans were nailed under the tabletop to accommodate liquor bought from the local peddler or from the base commissary and "smuggled" into the club. The club sold only ice and mixes. Every evening at about nine there would be an announcement that the inspector would be coming shortly and all liquor must be off the table. The liquor bottle went into the ubiquitous juice can and the inspector accepted an envelope from the management as he left.

My tenure in service was winding down and the process of my self-improvement still remained. Again I was blessed with a few devoted and well-educated friends who bolstered my determination to pursue an education. I took a few correspondence courses and continued to read whenever possible. Due to the convivial nature of our particular group it was difficult to stay on task. Off duty hours were spent in town at a favorite "watering hole" or on various excursions. A few were inspirational but most were just plain fun.

On base duties continued to include flights about the country and arduous training missions that were at best tedious. As my air force tenure began to wind down I received a letter inviting me to apply to the Air Force Cadets School. Acceptance would mean an officers rank after graduation. It was intriguing and offered another option for advancement.

Months before discharge the company CO was required to give you three recruitment talks. The first meeting went well. I described my plan to try for college acceptance and failing that goal I would apply to Cadets or reenlist if conditions seemed favorable. He agreed it was a good plan and would bother me no further and offered help if needed.

It was time for me to get serious about the future. On an informational level I felt equal to most of my peers and I certainly had matured both socially and intellectually. My interests had broadened and I had come to grips with what avenues I could realistically pursue. The most practical course would be to attend Emory Riddle Aeronautical School and get licensed as an A&E mechanic. My favorite career choice would have been to become a psychologist. Further down the list was an interest in photography requiring study at the New York School of Photography. My last choice was to become a teacher of manual arts, which was the original intent when I enlisted in the Air Force.

I had joined the service to qualify for the GI Bill. The World War Two GI Bill provided tuition, books, and a one hundred-dollar a month stipend. By the time my tour of duty ended only the stipend was available. This of course limited the real choices.

The decision I made was based on simple economics. By working summers as a carpenter along with the stipend the only realistic choice was a four-year college degree at a very inexpensive state college.

I began the search. My girl friend encouraged me to try Oklahoma A&M which offered a teaching degree. They were very interested and were willing to make a verbal commitment. Fitchburg State College in Massachusetts was interested and requested I set up an interview. I did.

I asked the CO for a week's leave to attend the interview. I intended to hitch hike both ways. He checked the outgoing military flights and got me a ride to Cleveland. From there I hitch hiked home. After a few short rides I then got a ride by a guy delivering two cars to a dealer in NJ. We traveled Route 20 all the way to Springfield, MA. A trucker delivering strawberries to Boston provided the next lap of my journey. We dined on strawberries all the way to Route 3. I had not eaten in two days and my stomach warned of an impending problem. When he let me off I made an emergency stop over the embankment and then continued home.

Before going to Fitchburg I went to visit my principal and mentor at Lowell Trade School who was overjoyed to see me. I explained my intention to try to enroll at Fitchburg. He was so happy that tears rolled down his cheeks. After he composed himself he asked if I would consider Terra Haute State College in Indiana as an alternative. I shrugged. He phoned the dean of men at Terra Haute who happened to have roomed with him at Holy Cross College. My praises were sung and I was accepted. He wasn't done he called my old coach and teacher and I was to return the next day and learn how to be interviewed. He also made a transcript of my grades. As I previously noted academics was not what one went to trade school for. The transcript process went like this: " Can you calculate the area of a rectangle?" "Yes." "Can you determine the number of board feet in a piece of lumber?" "Yes." "That's Plane Geometry." "A". "Can you figure out rafter and stud layout with the framing square?" "Sure." "Trigonometry." "A."

My transcript looked good. In those days if you were in the upper quadrant of your class you did not need to take the SATs. The principal's recommendation along with your transcript sufficed for most state colleges.

The following day I went before the college interviewing board consisting of a group of older professors. I fielded all questions and felt full of confidence. The question that sealed my acceptance evolved from my current status. They asked about my discharge and I told them that I was to be discharged in two months. I was currently stationed in Oklahoma and was granted a leave to appear before the interviewing board. They asked if I had traveled by train. I told them of my journey and was asked when I was due back. I explained that I had four days to hitch hike back. They were impressed with my level of tenacity and said I would receive a letter with their decision within a month. When I got back to base three days later my letter of acceptance was waiting. I had left the base the previous week with twenty-eight dollars in my pocket and I returned with sixteen.

In 1954 it was easy to hitch a ride when in uniform. The first lap was pleasant and uneventful and left me beyond Schenectady, NY. I was then offered a ride with two heavily intoxicated men driving in a new Dodge convertible. They offered me a lift to Toledo, OH if I would drive. We checked the map and determined that it was doable. I drove all night as they slept. They would awaken periodically and insisted I should eat. At the first stop I agreed to a hamburger. The most inebriated of the pair insisted I needed a steak and apple pie. We ate and continued on. That event was to occur twice more during the trip. In Erie, PA the state police stopped us and the two inebriates awakened as I was explaining the situation to the officer. The owner was asked for his registration. He became belligerent and made some profane observations about the officer's parentage and methods of copulation. As the officer walked around the vehicle the owner of the car fell back to sleep and proceeded to snore. The policeman came back to my door and returned my license and I promised not to err again. He let us go. About noon we neared Toledo and parted. I caught several more rides dropping down from Route 20 to Route 40 leading to St. Louis.

On Route 40 I was picked up by a GI from Kentucky who was on his way to an army base in Oklahoma. I was to share the driving but he made the mistake of offering me some moonshine. It looked like water and was so smooth I misjudged its potency. When I awoke we were near Tulsa, Oklahoma.

The CO was prepared to offer a signing bonus of two thousand dollars and a promotion if I re-enlisted. That was an enticing sum of money to me. He never pushed the issue and assured me I was making the right decision.

When I was discharged I drove my Plymouth Concorde first to Detroit to visit an old air force friend and his wife for a few days and then headed east. I got as far as Buffalo before my car was hit broadside at an intersection. My car rolled over twice before wrapping around a maple tree. Both drivers survived. I had multiple bruises and a serious gash in my back. After a visit to the hospital the police set me up in a small local hotel. The next morning I awakened and couldn't move. About eleven the maid came in and I asked for some ice. She came back with the manager who had been apprised of the situation. My leg was badly swollen. After applying lots of ice I was able to move about but was in serious pain. I called home and told my mother I had car trouble and would be delayed. She and my father had lived in Buffalo previously for many years, she had a close friend there and I stayed a week with them until I could walk. It wasn't bad duty. They had a beautiful granddaughter who was my companion for the week.

I finally reached home and started school in September although I still could not sit down without residual pain.

Back in New England with friends, 1955

Chapter Eleven

Education and Change

Without a great deal of fanfare I arrived home. Thanks to accumulated leave time, travel expense money and the insurance check for my car I had enough money to start college.

The biggest problem I had was an inability to sit properly due to an unresolved clot on my derriere caused by the accident. The drive from Lowell to Fitchburg was about thirty uncomfortable miles.

The second difficulty revealed itself in the form of the math class to which I was assigned. Thanks to the transcript my principal had developed based on shop math and arithmetic I was placed in an advance group that went from algebra through differential calculus in two semesters. I was dumfounded. I had never had a course in algebra and have difficulty spelling calculus. I got through those courses due to a sympathetic professor. Every afternoon after class I would go back to the professor and she would help me muddle through assignments. It was not a great ego builder.

The rest of the curriculum was within reasonable limits. I was well ahead of many of my classmates in most of the shops due to prior experience in woodworking and mechanics. I really enjoyed the academic classes with the exception of the math experience. I read every book and turned in every assignment on time. Most of the courses were new adventures to me and I was happy to be involved in what was offered. The other students often hated courses in philosophy, economics and even music appreciation; I couldn't believe my luck to be able to add these areas to my repertoire.

The social life was good also. There were basically three student groups: the veterans, the non-veterans, and the girls. Each group had its own agenda. The veterans tended to be mature and could legally drink. Much of their entertainment took place off campus whereas the non-vets used the campus facilities more frequently as did the girls. There was also the commuting group who spent the least amount of time on campus. The commuters were well accepted and when the occasion arose that warranted staying over there was always space available in a friend's dorm room.

College went well for me. I was just another student with no baggage attached. I felt great about myself and developed a measure of popularity. After the first year I made the dean's list with some regularity and made my mother proud.

During the summer months I worked as a carpenter. My goal was to save eight hundred to a thousand dollars to supplement the one hundred ten dollars a month from the GI Bill. The contractors knew my situation and allowed me plenty of overtime. All went well until the end of my sophomore year when my parents announced that they were closing the house and moving into a subsidized housing project. My father had retired and money was tight.

I decided to take a year off and work in order to raise money. I announced this decision to my commuting companion. He was as disappointed as I was. The next day I was invited to move in with his family. I would pay the same rent, ten dollars a week, and do some long needed repairs to his house. I started my junior year uninterrupted. It worked out well. He got his porch enclosed, doors hung, repairs made and I continued my education.

Each year we had to take an elective subject. The custom was to take an easy course and coast through it. I wanted to take something beneficial so I went to the science department and enrolled in a course called meteorology. The professor refused me as I was not a science major and I didn't have the prerequisites. I went to the dean and he forced her to accept me. I bought the text and started class. It didn't sound like the class I had expected. I was prepared to learn about meteorites. All she talked about was weather. It finally dawned on me that meteorology was the study of weather. I never was a great speller. I was able to hide my ignorance, however, and did well in the course. I was well acquainted with weather maps and all the terminology except for the word meteorology. The Air Force never used that word. We called it the weather forecast. When I crewed in a B-25 I had often enjoyed sitting in the glass nose photographing cloud formations. I never knew they were actually cumulonimbus, cirrus and stratus.

In the spring of my junior year I had fixed a close friend up with a girl who had already graduated from the nursing program at Fitchburg and was currently teaching in the program affiliated with the college. We went to visit her one weekend where she lived with two other nurses.

I knew only one of them and was introduced to the others. One was a very shy and attractive girl with long brown hair. We talked for some time and the others mentioned that she was a good cook. They raved about her spaghetti and so I invited my friend and myself to dinner the following Saturday. It was agreeable and she has continued cooking for me for the last forty-three years.

We began dating and by the late fall we were thinking of marriage although I never remember proposing in the traditional sense. Money was tight. I was stashing my summer wages in order to meet my expenses for my senior year. I moved into the dorm during my last year at Fitchburg. It was a new experience and afforded Ezaura and I more time together.

When we decided to get married we went to Lowell to meet my parents. It was a brief encounter where everyone tried not to appear uncomfortable. This was an uncommon event in our household and we all muddled through it.

A few weeks later we visited her parents in Fairview, MA where we spent the weekend. They had a two-bedroom house that her father had built. It was very comfortable and on a large private lot.

When it came time to retire I became somewhat anxious about the arrangements. The sofa was the obvious solution but it seemed to be small. I need not have worried her parents had the solution. I slept in a room with her father and she slept with her mother. I tried desperately not to snore.

On a subsequent weekend when we were again visiting her parents they had an evening engagement. We were expecting a few private moments but that was not to be. Their ten-year old granddaughter appeared as they were leaving. She was to be our duenna for the evening.

Her father was building a house on speculation on a lot that he owned. He worked as a machinist by day and built the house in his spare time. He had hired a carpenter to shingle the roof. He had been at it for two weeks and had four rows of shingles laid. Her father was discouraged. I offered help telling him we could easily finish the roof on the following weekend. He agreed saying we could go as far as possible and he would finish it during the week. The next weekend the roof was finished well before Ezaura and I left for Fitchburg. I declined his offer of compensation. After all he was to become my father-in-law. As we were leaving he stuffed something in my pocket. Later I discovered it was a fifty-dollar bill. I had never seen one before.

Ezaura insisted she did not need an engagement ring. She got one anyway. Her father had paid for half of it already. She didn't object too strenuously. She did have to spring for the marriage license however. Our wedding date was set for February 15th, 1958.

I got an unfurnished apartment near the college for the last semester. My wife-to-be was living in the next town with her friends. When we could get together we would attempt to gather furnishings for the apartment.

We were told of a furniture warehouse on Canal St. in Boston that was reasonable. I spent my last three hundred dollars for our bedroom set. The rest of our furnishings included a five-dollar couch from the Goodwill Store as well as a random collection of household surpluses from friends and family.

As the wedding grew closer friends threw us a surprise party and everything was progressing as planned.

We both had cars although my forty-seven Plymouth coupe was shamefully deficient. Ezaura drove a nice 1950 Buick Sedan that was the obvious choice for our honeymoon vehicle. That was the plan until she was side swiped on a narrow, slippery country road lined with snow embankments.

We had both exhausted all our funds and it was too late to have her car repaired. My old roommate had bought a new VW Bug and he insisted we use his car and he would use mine during the planned trip. Another friend's aunt owned a nice motel in the Berkshires and rented us a room for 25 dollars for the week.

By the time the wedding date had arrived we had both agreed to forgo the honeymoon idea and go back to Fitchburg after the wedding. The wedding went well. We both remembered our lines "I do" and proceeded to the Portuguese Club for the reception. There were three complete entrees: roast beef, followed by ham and then turkey. Cases of beer, wine and liquor were piled high behind the bar. The band played, people danced and chatted and reveled until long after we left.

I had never attended an ethnic wedding before. The guests kept coming up to congratulate me and would hand me a card. This went on for some time. My pockets and hands were full. I finally caught Ezaura's eye and complained. She indicated I should endure the custom and got me a container for the rest of the cards.

We left the celebration and went back to her house to change into street clothes. It was then that I realized that the cards contained money totaling nearly two thousand dollars. I couldn't believe it. The honeymoon was on again.

We settled into the honeymoon suite. Ezaura was not feeling well. She had a fever. I summoned a doctor. "Strep throat" he said; and gave her some medication and left. Starting a family would have to wait. She insisted that I should go skiing as planned. I felt badly but dared not cross her. I skied for a few hours and brought comestibles and nursed her back to health She recovered in a few days though her throat remained sore. We dined well and enjoyed the trip as best we could.

We returned to Fitchburg and started life together. A classmate's uncle owned an auto repair shop. He let me use his shop to replace the necessary undercarriage parts. Paying for the parts was my only expense.

I graduated on schedule and we moved to Western Massachusetts where I had been offered a job teaching Industrial Arts in Springfield.

Chapter Twelve
More Education More Change

College life ended and I had my bachelor's degree. Friends and foes alike shook their collective heads in disbelief. I reveled in their agony. Ezaura and I moved into a pleasant apartment in Holyoke and even bought a few pieces of new furniture. Ezaura quickly found employment at Holyoke Hospital. She worked there until the end of the year.

I started teaching Industrial Arts in Springfield that fall. My self-confidence and general status among my peers improved. Life was good. My first year salary was three thousand six hundred dollars that was below the poverty level. The future, however, looked promising.

My father-in-law told us about a lot on his street that was for sale for five hundred dollars. We liked it. It had five aging oak trees and was a corner lot. He knew we didn't have the money and offered to buy the lot and we could repay him in the future. We got a building loan for eight thousand dollars. Being a veteran I could get a loan at 41/2 %. Life looked rosier. We spent the summer building. I worked seven long days a week all summer.

My father-in-law worked with me every evening, weekend and during his vacation.

I started teaching in the fall and continued to work on the house weekends and evenings usually with my father-in-law who had now become "Pa". We worked well together and later built three more houses.

We moved into our mostly finished new home in the late fall of '58. Ezaura was getting somewhat heavy with child by then and I was adjusting well to my new career as a teacher. When the house was completed the bank transferred the funds remaining in our mortgage account to our checking account. We now had eight hundred left over in the bank, a house of our own and a baby on the way. Good Lord! Who would have predicted such a positive outcome? We still owed Pa five hundred for the lot. We put money aside each month. By late spring we ceremoniously and proudly marched across the street and paid our debt. He was furious. He was attempting to give us the money but didn't know how. We had ruined his ploy.

William was born on the sixth of February 1959. It was a difficult birth for his mother. She had carried him for nearly ten months and he had prospered in her womb. She has since forgiven him however. While I was trying to identify him through the nursery window another couple was also searching for their kin. The guy observed one infant and remarked, "Look at that one. He looks like he got hit in the face with a shovel". He had located our first-born. He had forceps marks on his face, a red flat nose, bulging eyes and a misshapen head. He grew up fine and healthy and shamelessly claims to be the best looking of the entire brood.

A year later William's first brother was born. Unfortunately he only survived a few days. The next month would be the most traumatic time of our lives. I attempted to go back to work after a week but couldn't get through the first hour. My understanding principal sent me home and arranged for an extended leave of absence that was much appreciated. The experience was very sorrowful and is rarely referred to.

When our third child was born we were very apprehensive. Fortunately we got it right this occasion and continued to do so from then on.

Justin was the biggest of all our offspring at birth. His mother was getting more experienced and he fared much better than his older brother. When I saw him through the window he was easy to pick out. The other two babies were black.

We had decided to move to Springfield where I was teaching. We signed the papers for the house the morning of the day Justin was born. We had sold our first house at a profit and now had money in the bank.

Our feeling was that the school system looked more favorably on staff members that lived in the community. We learned quickly that, though this was a factor, political connections ruled. This was something I was not good at and in fact found it somewhat distasteful.

The faculty where I taught was a close-knit group. We all got along well professionally and socially. I taught there for four years and the friendships I made at that time have endured forty-five years.

By the time I was transferred to another school I had earned a Master's Degree in counseling from Westfield State College. I was also very active in the teachers' union and that was not looked upon with favor by the administration. Union members were a troublesome element. They tended to question authority and instigate for higher wages. The fact was that we always operated within the rules and were a congenial lot and that irritated them all the more.

My next assignment was a predominately black junior high school in the "inner city". Though at first I was apprehensive it turned out to be the best teaching experience of my career. The student body was indeed tough, somewhat loud but at the same time warm and friendly. They were good judges of character and could assess whether you were for or against them. As a teacher you could be tough and demanding as long as they felt were fair. A sense of humor helped the situation as well as an interest in sports. When I was transferred I volunteered to assist the coach during wrestling season. We would often practice on Saturday morning. William was about five years old and would accompany me to the workouts. The toughest kids on the team would challenge him to wrestle. They would fall to the mat with William pouncing on them. Feigning defeat and pleading for mercy brought the match to an end.

The faculty there was also a close knit and friendly group. The administration was supportive. The main concern was the quality of what took place in the classroom. What I did registered well at the top and made the teaching experience a rewarding one. I was teaching wood shop, it was always my strongest area of interest. Previously I had taught classes in printing, machine shop, and mechanical drawing none of them would have been my choice.

At the same time I was still trying to broaden my background. Feelings of insecurity on the academic level still haunted me.

At the same time when I was reading the recent existential writers; such as, Sartre and Genest as well as developing an interest in Broadway musicals, an incident occurred that impacted my developmental mind-set.

One day at lunch several teachers were sitting at a table next to mine. They were the intellectually elite of our faculty. Their discussion involved a current Broadway play but they couldn't pinpoint the author or the name of the play. I turned to them and said, "that sounds like Genest's <u>From the Balcony</u>". They looked at me in stunned silence and agreed that that was correct. The lowly shop teacher had the answer. Another time they were discussing the origin of "My Fair Lady" which Ezaura and I had recently seen on Broadway. Again I was able to help them. " It was based on Shaw's "<u>Pygmalion</u>", I offered. Again it was met with disbelief.

I started to become smugly comfortable within myself and at the same time realized that I had made significant progress. I also realized that as long as I was the shop teacher I might be able to make an impression but I would always be " the shop teacher".

126

It was necessary to get serious about changing my career goals in order to satisfy my inner feelings of legitimacy. The next semester I enrolled at the University of Massachusetts in an advanced master's degree program in educational counseling and psychology known in education as the "sixth level certification.

I did well. A professor new to the university was impressed with a paper I had developed. I consisted of a stratified sample determining how teachers viewed psychological I Q test results. We jointly submitted it for publication to " The Clearing House Review" and it was accepted. It was a first publication for both of us.

I must admit at this point that all through grad school where most every course required a paper I was at the mercy of my editor who just happened to be my wife. Though I did the research and knew what to say and how to say it my grammatical and spelling skills left much to be desired. It is needless to say that although I have improved somewhat nothing I write is ever seen in print without my editor's scrutiny. If you are not having difficulty reading this work remember to thank her.

After being granted the advanced graduate certification I enrolled in the doctoral program. In order to matriculate it was necessary to pass the Miller's Analogy

Test at a prescribed level. I had developed a reasonably strong vocabulary but drawing analogies was foreign to me. It was worrisome but that hurdle was cleared by a reasonably good margin. Several others with stronger educational backgrounds, one of whom was to become my boss ten years later, did not fare as well and were rejected.

The doctoral faculty, though small, was diverse. It included professors with psychological commitments to Rogers, Skinner, or the directive approaches in the use of psychology that reflected the most prevalent theories at the time.

The tenets of Carl Rogers interested me the most. When each class was over it was common for a group of us, including the professor, to adjourn to our favorite watering hole in Amherst and rehash previous discussions. More was learned there than was possible in the classroom setting.

The Springfield School System had granted me a sabbatical leave at half pay for the nineteen sixty-six school-year. Up until that time all my studies had been in the afternoon/evening and during the summer months. In order to pursue a doctorate a full year of on campus study was necessary.

During the fall of sixty-six we rented our house in Springfield and moved on campus at U Mass into the married student-housing compound. It was a good experience. William and Justin attended school in Amherst. Andrea was a year old. During the fall we bicycled about the area. Andrea rode on the back of her mother's bike and Justin rode with me. William rode his own bike with a rope tied to the handlebars the end laid on his shoulder. When we came to a difficult hill I would ride by him, take the rope and help him up the hill. On spring weekends we would visit the farm animals as the young were being born.

The university had granted me an assistantship. The stipend was $280 a month, a welcome addition to the sabbatical leave funds we received.

I was assigned to the acting dean for the school of education and served as his assistant. I would also substitute for various professors when they could not meet their classes. It was a great experience. The dean was a great human being and a strong advocate for my progress.

My initial thoughts were that I certainly was in over my head. Luckily they were unfounded. I developed a great relationship with the dean and was involved in tasks that I never imagined possible from teaching class segments, screening doctoral candidates, editing the superintendents association's quarterly publication, to arranging meetings and conferences.

I was elected to Phi Delta Kappa, an honorary society of graduate educators, eventually serving as president. I later became the delegate to the national convention that met annually in cities throughout the country. The membership of the general assembly consisted of about two thousand delegates from colleges and universities, as well as school superintendents and educators.

Later, in the early seventies, I attended the annual meeting in Louisville, KY. On the agenda was a motion to offer membership to qualified female educators. I attended the convention with instructions from the university chapter to support inclusion. After two days of debate, a motion passed to allow female membership on a local option basis. As soon as order was restored I rose on a point of personal privilege and asked for immediate reconsideration. After a brief parliamentary recess it was granted. I offered a substitute motion allowing full inclusion arguing now that the organization had accepted the premise of equality; there was an obligation to provide full membership access. Our side won after an enthusiastic but briefer debate. The membership of the university was pleased with the outcome and the earth continued to rotate.

The school of education was in the process of undergoing a total transformation. A well-known education reformer was hired from California to head the school. He brought with him a whole new faculty and a cadre of doctoral candidates. They were an extremely liberal bunch that preferred tee shirts and jeans to shirts and ties. Western Massachusetts tended to. Be more conservative and traditional and didn't adapt well to the change in customs. Most of the old faculty moved on to the more traditionally oriented schools.

I was getting to the dissertation stage of my program. The advisor that was assigned me had no interest in the areas that I wanted to pursue. He attempted to interest me in an avant-garde teaching approach right out of the theater of the absurd. I was to be the researcher. It was so ridiculous that there was nothing to measure in a research format. The program became so shallow that I opted out. I had learned a great deal at the university and my inner strength allowed me to walk away from the situation that I had become dissatisfied with without guilt. My mother was disappointed but I think my over worked editor was secretly pleased.

Ezaura was carrying our final contribution to the population explosion, as we were about to return to Springfield. On the day before we were to move back to our house in Springfield, we rented a box van and left our car in the truck rental lot. Ezaura and I then drove the truck back to Amherst. We had already organized a group of friends to help load our furniture on the following day.

At one AM Ezaura awakened me and announced that she had to go to the hospital "NOW". "Can't you wait until we load the truck in the morning?" I pleaded. "Now", she repeated. I was aware that a bumpy twenty-mile ride in the moving van would undoubtedly exacerbate the birthing process that I was unprepared to handle. After arousing my next-door neighbor he lent me his car and his wife watched over the sleeping kinder. We made it. I returned to Amherst.

That morning as my friends and I were midway through loading the van the phone rang. The doctor announced the birth of our son, Brandon. As I am now approaching 70, I am quite sure that he will be our last.

Interestingly he has the same birthday as his great grandfather and that is within four days of his grandfather. He also shares the same birth date as his nephew, Jonathan who is William's son.

Chapter Thirteen

Making Headway

When I returned to my teaching assignment I was well received. The principal had moved on and his successor and I were very compatible. During the sabbatical year the substitute had had his share of difficulty with the more troublesome students. The wood shop was in poor repair and the new regime had introduced a course combining small engine repair and electric circuit boards. A great deal of money had been spent on the new program and the administration was so proud of it that I had not the heart to tell them how seriously they had erred. The equipment consisted of ten circuit boards and ten lawn mower engines. No manuals were ordered and there was one set of tools available to the entire class. Student interest was low. There were no lawns in the inner city. The prevailing attitude was, "Why do we need to learn this?" We managed to muddle through the year. We still had the wood shop and it was offered in exchange for their tolerance.

The students welcomed me back with good humor and I was happy to be back. Our rapport had always been good. It was my practice to keep the shop open for an hour after school ended. Students would return to work on their projects and to talk. Good behavior in all classes was the price of admission. If another teacher complained about missing assignments or there was detention, they would have to fulfill those responsibilities before they could return.

The students' woodworking talent showed exceptional promise. I made arrangements at a local downtown bank for an exhibit. The pieces consisted of a good assortment of well-made projects, cobbler's benches, chess tables, and bookcases, each with the maker's name on display. The school was happy and the boys were proud. One of the craftsmen was extremely proud of his work. While carrying his table home he stopped at a neighborhood variety store and the owner offered him twenty dollars for it. That was a handsome sum to this boy. He came to school the next day and proudly told us he turned down the offer. Others had similar experiences. Many of them were problematic students and the attention received wore well.

My personal confidence had peaked. I had come to accept what I knew and did not become embarrassed by data I had missed or had no interest in. Years of curiosity about the arts and literature had allowed me to feel comfortable in a variety of areas that fostered an air of intelligence. Avoiding areas of intellectual weakness such as math or the sciences without feeling guilt developed with maturation.

The university experience was particularly broadening. I was surrounded by a group of very astute students and dedicated professors and was accepted without question.

Within a few years of my return to the classroom I began to apply for positions in counseling and psychology. The major hurdles turned out to be political rather than academic. Credentials were a secondary factor. What were needed were four votes from the school committee. Votes could be garnered through personal contact or by an administrator's intervention.

I had spent many years developing my character as somewhat of a maverick. Administrators don't often look for more problems and I barely knew the names of the school board members. I preferred to be recognized on the merits of accomplishment and contribution.

Fortunately the first principal I had worked for came to the rescue. He had become the Assistant Superintendent of Pupil Services. We also had a new superintendent whom I had met at several academic venues in Atlantic City and at the university. I had never annoyed either of them and they were both aware of a few positive attributes in my favor. Though I had applied for a counselor's position the two top administrators determined that I was better prepared to be a school psychologist and offered me a position that opened up. I accepted gratefully and remained in that position for the next twenty-five years.

The principal, counselors, and teachers were receptive. Our department was evolving. Where once schools were accustomed to receiving only IQ scores they would now receive an analysis of the data from a variety of instruments and observations. We also were available to the staff and parents. I really enjoyed parental interaction. Many parents had an interest in evolving change in their family management styles but were often too overwhelmed to be effective.

There were the occasional bumps in the pathway but professionally and privately outcomes progressed smoothly. Unfortunately my colleagues were aware of my proclivity to play the contrarian at professional meetings and would often bait me into controversy. An avid supporter once observed, "Howie could be kneeling at the altar praying and cause someone to take umbrage." It was a good analysis of my character though not a consistent one.

The immediate supervisor I was assigned to upon becoming a school psychologist was a fretting contrarian. His choice would have been anyone but me. He went so far as to apologize to several principals for assigning me to their schools. Within a few months they were singing my praises.

One day he called me into his office for a private consultation. He was aware that I had several publications and was conducting a statewide conference at the University on racial prejudice. He clearly expressed his concern that I was hurting myself by publishing and with my involvement at the University. The implication he proffered was that I knew more than the supervisory staff and that they would take umbrage. It became clear that he was feeling threatened. He had nothing to fear. He had been retired for ten years before I took his job that was twenty years after that meeting.

A new assistant superintendent was appointed. We were well acquainted. He was aware I had done some writing and was cognizant of the various departmental functions under his management. There had never been a compendium of the missions and responsibilities of each sector. Each was an individual fiefdom. I was asked to develop a descriptive manual of the programs offered by each department and how to access them. When the task was finally completed a year later it contained about ninety pages of copy with appropriate artwork in book form. Thousands of copies were printed and distributed. It was extremely well received. The state department asked for copies and they were distributed around the state. I have yet to receive acknowledgement for my effort.

Chapter Fourteen

Work and Family

During the summer months of the first five years of our marriage my father-in-law and I built several houses on speculation. The money earned kept us debt free and afforded us short vacation trips. Ezaura and I went to New York with friends and saw a good variety of Broadway plays. Those were good times that opened up insights to a whole new culture.

As our family began to develop we turned to camping as an affordable vacation venue. By this time we had sold our first home and bought a 1963 Mercedes diesel sedan. Although some thought it somewhat pretentious the idea was to buy a car that could be driven for many years. The cost was about the same as a Buick {$4300} or the equivalent cost of three Volkswagens depending on how you analyzed it. It served us well for thirteen years and 200,000 miles. We once traveled from Springfield to Orlando FL and paid more in tolls then we spent on diesel fuel at forty miles per gallon. Initially we would load our gear into a three by six-foot box atop the car. We usually traveled upward to four weeks or more depending on summer school or business obligations.

We enjoyed vacationing in the Eastern Provinces of Canada and on one occasion we went as far west as Winnipeg, Manitoba to visit a classmate who was teaching at the University. Later we ventured as far as Yellowstone National Park and the Tetons. All were great experiences.

Tenting became a thing of the past on one fateful trip to the Laurentides in Canada. It was damp and cold on this August trip and our youngest was at the crawling stage. The cold and mud at the campground were being tolerated until the small flies ate a ring around the infant's eyes. His mom had had enough.

Several years later she reluctantly agreed to a tent trailer. The family was growing up and the increased comfort it provided set us in motion again for a few more years of wandering about the country.

In order to take our brood out of the heat and stifling atmosphere of the crowded city neighborhood we decided to spend the summer in Wells, Maine in the tent trailer complete with screened tent cook house and shared bathrooms with strangers. The family made new friends readily and had the advantage of miles of beaches to roam and marshes to explore.

To afford this "luxury" I had taken a job as a carpenter. Their mother herded the offspring to and from the beach on their bicycles and generally tended to all our needs.

One evening Ezaura and I were strolling through a nearby neighborhood and happened to discover a lot for sale. It turned out to be affordable much to our surprise. Thus began a new phase in our lives.

Ten years earlier we had visited friends in Connecticut who subsequently moved west. They lived at that time in a carriage house in Pine Orchard that is located on Long Island Sound. We would amble through the neighborhood replete with the summer mansions of the idle rich wistfully thinking that it was unlikely that we would ever even own a simple vacation cottage.

Now we now owned a lot on a beautiful marsh just a five-minute walk to the ocean. The rest of the summer we spent constructing the house that was to become our "summer estate". Building the house was a joint effort. I had already designed a plan that we had intended to use for a new home in the Springfield area. It was adapted for our new summerhouse.

142

Construction began. The whole family cleared the lot during the day while I continued to work my carpentry job. Within a week the foundation hole was opened. We mixed cement for the footings and laid the blocks for the foundation. I would work evenings and weekends. My crew would work during the day and weekends as needed. Each evening I would assemble a section of the floor and stabilize the boards with a few nails. The day crew {family} would complete the nailing the next day. Within a month the entire shell of the house was up and boarded.

School was about to start and we all returned to Springfield with callused hands. We were now relegated to work only on weekends. My father-in-law became part of the labor force. Unfortunately for him he was a master of all trades. He was conscripted to install the plumbing and electricity while I shingled the roof, installed the windows, and finished the interior wall studs.

During the winter we kept busy and broke by watching and waiting for materials to go on sale that would be needed in the spring. Kitchen cabinets and doors were made in the cellar with the cheapest of materials with an eye toward upgrading these components in the future.

Throughout the early spring our oldest son and I would travel to Maine with materials. We would spend Saturday and Sunday clapboarding the outside of the house and insulating the walls. We slept in sleeping bags on mattresses donated during the winter by family and friends and haplessly froze waiting for the next morning. The house was barely habitable by summer but improved each day. By summer's end we were starting to enjoy our new digs.

During the next few summers we built two more houses on two of the four lots we had bought next to our house. We eventually sold both houses and the two lots and felt like veritable millionaires.

For the next fifteen summers I was a self-employed carpenter but would only work four to six hours a day. The older boys would help as needed yet still had time to enjoy the summer. It took twenty years before the summer cottage became a bona fide home. Additions and corrections still take place annually.

In the mean time our children developed into adults. All worked at summer jobs in restaurants or the grocery store as they became more self-reliant and independent. And so our lives went for many years. Our main residence was in Springfield where the family was schooled and I was employed.

I continued as a school psychologist until about 1990. The position of Supervisor of School Psychologists was posted. I was definitely interested. The school year ended. The position remained unfilled. During the summer at our home in Maine the phone rang. It was six-thirty in the morning. A voice claiming to be the personnel director announced that I was to be appointed to the position at the next board meeting. I laughed and was about to hang up. He convinced me not to. It was true.

I still had my protagonists and there were a few hard feelings. The most difficult part was dealing with my former peers. I had each fill out a list of preferred assignments. There were a few over-lapping preferences. Most all worked out amicably. As in any administrative situations there were occasions of disagreement. Publicly my people were always right. Attitude and relationship problems were handled privately usually with some success.

I enjoyed the new job though I spent considerably less time on evaluations. Most of my time evolved around parents, administrative tasks and the supervision of a host of related programs. These programs included the responsibility for after school tutors, home teachers, and nurses for the disabled and hospital tutors. At various times occasions would arise when other duties would be temporarily added to my domain such as speech pathology, vision and hearing testing and the like.

The school budget in most communities tends to grow as programs expand. New responsibilities are delegated to the institution and as the tax rate spirals upward the populous demands the cutting of the school budget. In our city this would often result in using attrition as a means of cutting personnel. After a supervisor retired or moved the duties would be divided among the remaining staff.

One of the reasons I decided on retirement, in addition to aging, was to avoid the inevitable situation where I would be supervising programs where I had no interest or limited skills. The apex of my career had been reached and it was time to go. I went.

Chapter Fifteen

Retirement

Time had run out. Retirement was at hand. About to retire, colleagues in our department honored us at an elegant and much appreciated party. Thirty-six years of continuous employment in various capacities had come to an end. New experiences were on the horizon and I approached them eagerly but with some reservation.

During the years leading up to retirement my wife and I had made plans that anticipated a change in lifestyle. In order to generate a feeling of accomplishment and hopefully add to the financial coffers I took up woodcarving. I had spent many years involved in various forms of woodworking from building houses to making furniture and teaching woodworking and felt that wood carving would be a natural adjunct. I took an evening adult course and continued to do so for several years. The techniques of woodcarving came easily to me. Many years of handling woodworking tools and machines proved to be a distinct advantage.

When the instructor retired he recommended that I take his place. I taught for upwards of ten years and enjoyed the experience tremendously. During this time I had developed a variety of bas-relief carvings as well as some carousel figures that were very popular. I built display racks anticipating an opportunity to sell carvings at fairs and craft shows.

Ezaura and I applied to a series of shows and I was accepted to most of them. We hit the road on weekends and achieved limited success. Within a short period of time show promoters began to invite us to exhibit at their fairs. They liked the fact that we were set up to demonstrate carving in our booth. We were often featured in their television and newspaper advertisements and on occasion we prospered. We were traveling further than we liked. We were doing shows in New York and New Jersey and even ventured into Washington, D.C. on a few occasions in addition to the New England States. The profits we garnered were used to upgrade our home in Maine in preparation for our eventual retirement.

Ezaura never enjoyed dealing with the masses at fairs and preferred to stay in the background and read. In an attempt to involve her more I made some animal figure blanks and encouraged her to carve. She now has her own set of tools and enjoys creating a menagerie that is usually given as gifts. When I finally retired we both had grown weary of the show business. We currently enjoy the leisurely life we have created and find many ways to keep busy. We both still enjoy carving but at a less demanding pace.

After the sale of our house in Springfield we moved to our summer home in Maine. We were disappointed that houses in the city were no longer selling at a premium. We ended up selling it for half of what we originally expected and are still surviving.

We had been vacationing in Arizona for a few weeks each winter for about ten years before retirement. Close friends had relocated there at the same time we were starting to develop our Maine home. We would go to Arizona to warm up each winter and they would come to Maine to cool off during the summer.

We were trying to figure out how to manage spending the winter in Arizona when our friends called us and offered a proposal we couldn't refuse. We were to stay with them for the winter in exchange for tiling floors in their house. We spent the winter in Arizona and loved it.

The next year we rented an apartment in Tempe, Arizona. The following winter we again stayed with our friends and did some odd jobs and repairs in addition to more tile setting.

In the course of our stay we visited friends in Sun City a well-planned retirement community. It was and is a very clean and safe environment with a variety of amenities such as; pools, golf courses and craft workshops of all kinds. After visiting a number of houses we decided to rent a house for the winter of the following year to determine whether we would like the area. We did.

We located a realtor and began house hunting. We found a house we liked. In the mean time our daughter and son-in-law proposed that they buy the house as an investment and rent it back to us. The rent was set at a remarkably affordable rate. We were to be caretakers and make improvements as we saw fit. We have been working on it for three happy seasons and hope to have it totally to our liking within a few more years.

While in Arizona as in Maine we continue a very active life. We make it a practice to take daily walks of four to five miles or more depending on our self-assigned tasks. We also like to hike in the surrounding mountains and take numerous side trips.

We have developed an interest in Native American Indian culture and have visited numerous Ancient Indian ruins throughout Arizona and New Mexico and a few in Colorado and Utah. We are quite captivated with their art as well.

Recently we acquired a Subaru Outback for easier access into the remote areas where the ancient ruins can be found. On a previous search for the Gila Indian Cliff dwellings we were unprepared for what turned out to be a forty-mile adventure into a National Forest. The road was rough in spots and we owned a Dodge Caravan. At times we feared the wheels would fall off. We made it safely but immediately began saving up for a Subaru which is intended for rugged off-road driving.

Earlier this year we hired an Indian Guide to show us the many ancient dwellings in Canyon de Muerto in Chinle, Arizona that is in the heart of the Navajo Nation. In April the mouth of the canyon is covered with winter water runoff several inches deep. Currents often occur that are masked by surface water. Fortunately our guide, a Navajo named Kenneth Watchman, knew the canyon well. He expertly guided us through the shallowest parts of many streams. On occasion, however we distracted him with conversation and entered deeper water. The hood of the Subaru dipped under water on four different occasions with nary a sputter. On the way out of the canyon we passed several jeeps and a commercial tour vehicle carrying unhappy tourists being towed to dry land. We waved as we passed by hoping to cheer them.

Though most people choose to fly to and from their winter retreats we prefer to drive. We intend to continue to do so until it becomes impractical. It is a great history lesson. We opt for different routes each time we journey and have covered a great deal of the country from east to west and from the Gulf coast in the south to Utah and Colorado in the north. We tend to avoid cold and snow laden routes.

So far the experiences have been largely positive. The general routes are planned with emphasis on the certain areas of interest we want to explore. Time schedules are loosely adhered to.

To grasp the vastness of the country one must drive through it. The farms and cattle ranges of the west leave us in awe due to their size. A full day of driving does not bring us to the end of the grasslands. Farmland extends into the horizon and beyond on both sides of the highway. Another days drive with no end in sight. The terrain is always in a state of flux. The hardship of the pioneer life becomes a reality. Here lies the simplicity and beauty of the land that feeds and nurtures us. The transportation system composed of long trains and trucks is constantly on the move eternally laden with the products that we take for granted.

The raw beauty of the mountains and forests can only be fully appreciated when viewed. The finest photographs of Ansel Adams are beautiful and inspiring but even he would admit {I think} that the panorama and sounds could not be replicated in a picture.

Though neither my wife nor I really enjoy driving through major cities their organization and superstructure boggle the mind. I personally prefer the architecture and simplicity of the older historic sections of cities and towns rather than the new skyscrapers. When we travel through New Mexico, for example, we often seek out the old towns with the original adobe houses still in use after hundreds of years.

Driving does have its perils however. Leaving Napa Valley in California heading east to our summer home in Maine one year we were about to encounter a major set back. Entering the legendary Donner Pass and continuing through the mountains defy any hope of adequate description. From there you enter Nevada and drive hundreds of miles through less spectacular landscapes with a quiet beauty and relaxed atmosphere.

Another terrain change occurs in Utah. Here you encounter the Bonneville Salt Flats about a hundred miles of barely habitable land, not particularly beautiful, but a natural phenomenon we often hear about. The scene changes abruptly after leaving Salt Lake City. Here you begin to enter a mountainous area where coal mining is a major resource. A panorama of ten thousand foot mountains completes a setting where few towns can exist. Our transmission took umbrage and stuck in third gear. Sixty miles to the only town with a transmission repair shop. Two days later and fourteen hundred dollars poorer we continued our journey east. We crossed Mid-America with little confidence. The transmission failed again in Pennsylvania. We limped home to Maine in third gear after a surly transmission shop owner couldn't find time to talk to us. We bought the Subaru Outback.

Returning to Maine each year is like returning home after an extended journey. Although we have happily adapted to our home in Arizona and thoroughly enjoy our life there we are undoubtedly New Englanders at heart. The long walks on the beach, the nightly ocean breezes, proximity to family and life long friends are highly anticipated. How could we abandon the house and property that took thirty years to complete and the garden that will soon yield fresh vegetables throughout the summer and the yearly battle we always lose to the marauding woodchucks, moles and in the fall the deer. We can't, which is why we return each spring.

In due time the leaves will turn heralding the onset of a colder, less hospitable environment for these old bones and we will again complete the cycle by returning to Arizona. Our intention is to continue this cycle as long as our health allows. We view a nomadic life style as sharing in the best of both worlds

Chapter Sixteen

My Perspective

At this juncture I am fast approaching seventy. Life prior to my third year of existence seems to have failed the test for a normal pattern of a child's development. Parental nurturing was non-existent. I was obviously an unwelcome interlude that interfered with the life style of a parent who never wanted the responsibility of raising a family. Her problem was undoubtedly compounded by poverty and limited patience for a child who required continual medical attention. She solved her problem by boarding her progeny with strangers and finally abandoning her responsibility entirely by absconding with the forces of justice at her heels.

Though it may appear incongruous I hold no ill will toward the architect of my early development. I have no memory of those early years. I am grateful that I was blessed with a faulty memory. It has served me well.

My earliest recollection of life began to develop when I was placed with the Cotes at the age of three. Although I was often gravely ill and needy in a variety of ways I cannot recall lamenting my human condition. It was the life experienced after that I remembered and it seemed normal to me. Life was good. I was extremely well cared for and protected. Everything I learned from proper manners and behavior to reading, writing and ciphering was the product of their teaching. All the bad stuff I learned later.

I was taught not to hate and to this day this concept is etched in my mind. That is not to say that I embrace everyone with equal ardor. I have encountered many people in my lifetime that I had difficulty relating to and vice versa. Differences in life styles, mores, and ideals are often encountered. People exist that I don't choose to fraternize with socially and I make a concerted effort to avoid but hatred is beyond my capacity. Hatred is a difficult feeling for most Americans to understand including myself. Most of us are unable to comprehend the ethnic and "religion" promoted malevolence that has endured for countless centuries in some countries. Though extreme cases in America exit much of the unpleasantness toward minorities is predicated on some form of fear. The fear of reduced value of our houses, job market erosion, and increased crime in the community to mention a few. We have experienced some progress on these issues in recent years and it will hopefully continue.

I have known prejudice in my life. State wards were often seen through a jaundiced eye. Many families discouraged their children from interacting with us. The community in general considered us "damaged goods" due to our questionable backgrounds. Parents were often less accepting than their children were. We fared much better on neutral territory, such as school or church. Everyone had a choice, they either liked you or they didn't, you could hit the ball or you couldn't. Simple choices were made. As we all matured bonds were formed on compatibility rather than family background.

My mother's nature was to respect others without exception. Her lesson for us was to "do good for bad". If someone was mean to you the best course of action was to "kill" him with kindness and make him ashamed of his unkind treatment of you. It rarely worked.

When I try to assess my progress in life I have difficulty viewing it as remarkable. Life continues to be a work in progress. Existence has always been a sequence of experiences of trial and error. Often many of the trials resulted in viable rewards that tended to temper the frequent errors in judgement. The progress made is often a matter of constant plodding hopefully in an upward trend.

An interesting phenomenon in life is the tendency of the healthy mind to recall the pleasant memories of the past. When a veteran is asked to share his wartime experiences rarely will you hear stories about the long frightful hours that he spent shivering in a wet foxhole, nor will you hear about charging the enemy with fixed bayonets to kill or be killed.

It is more likely that his story will describe the reception they all received during the liberation of Paris. These spicy memories will probably be the ones he never told his mother.

Work and Loyalty

It is difficult for me to understand the nature of the current employee/employer relationships. My generation was taught to work hard and well and engender a sense of loyalty to your employer and you would have a job for life. In today's job market a sense of loyalty to employer and employee has become a vague concept. Industries have grown so large and impersonal that staff is known only by its employee number. Workers have become so transient that, unlike the staff at "Cheers" on Beacon Street in Boston, nobody knows your name. Only the product has merit along with the bottom line.

I would have a great deal of difficulty with the uncertainty and lack of longevity in today's work environment. Planning for the future becomes a variable that I am happy not to have to consider.

Politics

I was raised in a working class family in the nineteen-thirties and everyone I knew was a Democrat. The most revered personalities during those difficult times were people such as Franklin D. Roosevelt who ushered us out of the great depression and a long list of union leaders who worked tirelessly for working people. The Catholic priests in our town extolled the virtue of supporting your union and voting at election time, hopefully for a Democrat.

When I was old enough to vote I voted for democrats, especially during national elections. In local elections I would often veer from the party line and vote for the individual. Local and state elections are more personal. Often times the candidate is known and it is easier to examine his or her performance. Such was my pattern of voting for many years.

I viewed government through liberal eyes at that time. The government existed to help us. The people needed support and the more entitlements the law provided the smoother the life would be for the masses. Eventually it became obvious that despite the best efforts of our government to improve the quality of life it was creating stagnation. The population we were trying to reach was losing its sense of purpose.

Over the last fifteen years I have gradually lost the liberal ideal. Unions have come under pressure and lost most of their impact. Government has taken itself much too seriously to the point where it has become the country's largest employer.

Those with the least experience with environmental factors bully politicians to enact senseless environmental laws that stunt the growth of energy plants and interfere with fuel distribution systems.

Liberal segments of the population who have rarely seen a forest or an animal in the wild promote legislation on environmental management and succeed. Our senators and representatives across the nation enact legislation on a variety of articles about which they know little and have no interest in the matter at hand. It often appears that their main objective is to look good and to hold on to their fabulous job in the next election. I am often amused while watching C-Span as a senator delivers an impassioned speech of the floor of the senate when no one is in attendance.

One might draw the erroneous conclusion that my view on politicians is somewhat negative. I do understand that they are a homogeneous group. There is an old saying that notes, "Cream always rises to the top of the bottle". It is unfortunate that the cream will sour if it hangs around too long. It is uncanny how often after a failed re-election campaign, the deposed legislator will be appointed to a job in the public domain.

Religion

When I became a ward of the State the hierarchy somehow determined that I was destined to become Catholic. The Cotes were an ecumenical family. They both were previously married. He was raised as a Catholic and she as a Protestant. Neither attended church though they lived their lives within the parameters of Christian ideals.

When I reached the age five it was determined that I needed to be baptized into the Catholic faith. My father became my godparent and I took his name as my baptismal middle name. I was named Howard William Marchie and would carry that name until I entered the Air Force in nineteen-fifty. At that time I sent for my birth certificate from the state department and learned that I had the middle name of Edgerton.

The Cotes dutifully raised me as a practicing Catholic. I received all the appropriate sacraments and attended catechism classes throughout the formative years. Ezaura and I raised our offspring as Catholics with marginal success.

I still consider myself a Christian with Catholic ideals although I have not been associated with a church for many years. I have reservations about some of the core rituals of the church and particularly dislike the changes in the Mass that have evolved over the last twenty years. I have always loved the choir and dislike the community sing-a-longs during Mass. The altar is not a stage. Please, get the band off the altar. The Mass was a continuous ritual. There is no need for an intermission for shaking hands, hugging or kissing the astonished parishioners around me. The Mass is normally less than an hour long, we can relate if we choose in the parking lot or community hall. The Mass is a formal event and should demand decorum.

I believe very strongly that the Ten Commandments are a perfect set of standards forming the framework by which civilized society can function successfully. They are the format within which I endeavor to live this imperfect life.

From time immemorial religious scholars have studied the various religions. Their interpretations are legion. Who is right? I have come to the conclusion that after years of catechism and many more years of listening to sermons I am ill equipped to reach conclusions when the most learned academics couldn't reach a consensus.

I have no idea what happens to us after death. Death may be final or it may be only phase one of an eternal venture. Hopefully if we live a worthy and productive life the final arbiter will be pleased and rule in our favor.

Research

Beware of what passes today as scientific research. Thanks to media involvement the word is practically synonymous with hype. The media has promoted phases of inquiry such as long-term weather predictions, a variety of polls as well as other social sciences, such as psychology and sociology as reliable sciences. When the questions involve how you feel or what you think there are too many variables that come into play that destroy the reliability of the data.

When I hear a reporter ask a professional what he thinks I become distrustful of the information he or she is about to utter. I care not what he/she thinks. I want insight as to what he actually knows. What he thinks is philosophy. What he knows are facts. The media also forces the early release of science in progress and treats it as a foregone conclusion raising the hopes of many people. The fact that the final conclusions could support the null hypothesis is rarely mentioned.

Marriage and Child Rearing

Shortly after I met Ezaura I knew the search was over. She was twenty-two and I was twenty-four when we married. The union has endured forty-four years with a minimum of agitation and a modicum of prosperity. Certainly there were times of disagreement but the problems we faced were not insurmountable.

The problems in marriages today are much the same as the difficulties previously described in the workplace and in society in general; a sense of loyalty and mutual commitment for a lifetime is essential. In our society half of the children in a family have grown up coping with multiple fathers or mothers due to divorce or single parenthood. I contend that the system of marriage as a lifetime venture is most profitable to all concerned. When discussing marriage inevitably the subject of sex must be explored. Sex was designed to be a mutually satisfying event made pleasurable to encourage family development. It was not the Designer's intent that the experience be used as a bargaining tool but rather as a vehicle of harmony.

I personally count myself among the lucky rejects of society who gained life from a union devoid of commitment and was salvaged by the caring and love of strangers.

Chapter Seventeen

As I See It

My focus in life has always been to engender the respect of my peers and to make progress toward achievable goals. The timetable I planned was often unrealistic and had to be modified. Academically I worked a great deal harder than most of my colleagues. I often feared that associates would discover that I was not as bright as I pretended to be.

When using the manual skills that I had developed over the years I was ardently dedicated to the task. The laziness I exhibited in my youth was no longer a factor. Actually it is all a sham. The reason I work hard is not that I love to work but rather an effort to finish quickly so that I can rest.

The mellowing effect of age has taught me that it takes a lifetime to complete a life. Coping seems to become easier with longevity. When I look back at issues that angered me to the point of reacting irrationally and reassess them in the present I feel foolish. It is now easier to decide what is not worthy of battle.

Aging seems to facilitate putting things into proper perspective. Concepts such as happiness and respect are not entitlements; they are earned rewards fostered by viable interactions and commitments. I like the thought Robert Service voiced in "The Creation of Sam McGee"; "A promise made is a debt unpaid". Fulfilling a promise is essential for developing trust.

While serving jury duty I had plenty of time to examine what life could have brought. If Freud had been totally accurate about the early formative years I would have been doomed. The sum of your experiences along with genetics, environment and personal interpretation will play the most significant role in defining what you will become.

My own experience encompassed gratefulness. I decided at an early age that I had miraculously found my "real" parents, the Cotes. Within our home I had lived with different state wards that could not make that decision.

I have come to believe that everything is how *you* see it. From emotionally based experiences conclusions develop. We tend to form opinions stemming from how we interpret our experiences. If in your mind you determine that the previous statement lacks merit than indeed it does. If the mind determines that all ---- ---- ---- should be eradicated justification can ensue.

The point of this profound observation is to try not to develop factual ideas based on personal prejudice. The world does not need any more Timothy McVeighs, Adolph Hitlers, or Osama Bin Ladens.

It is easy to get detached from society's developments as you age. I had the opportunity to be trained in the use of computers well before I retired. I rejected the idea. I wasn't ready to start amassing a whole new method of communicating. I liked the old tried and true systems. At the same time my wife loved the new concept and does well using it. Then again she *is* two years younger than I am.

We both agree that using phone menus, calling a business and talking to a computer is insane. This book would have begun two years earlier if we could have resolved the phone menu at the Massachusetts State Department.

We also cannot understand why people choose to wear the manufacturer's label on the outside of the clothing, or why they spend unreasonable amounts of money to advertise for Nike, Tommy Hilfger, etc. I've worn the clothing. They don't deserve the free advertising.

Lastly I have little affection for organizations like the EPA and other neo non-sciences as well as the entire lunatic fringe of urbanites that through their naivete and lack of knowledge are setting out to destroy my habitat.

I am willing to admit that I have a few shortcomings. I have been married to the same woman for forty-four years. It has taken me forty years to remember those two magic words, "Yes dear". I have also added "If it would please you, dear" and "what ever you say", without gritting my teeth. If I can learn it you can. Hopefully it will take less time.

This is the world according to Howard as I see it. Believe it or not these beliefs and experiences have served me for seventy years with a modicum of success.

Howard Edgerton Marchie, BHB*

*Basic Human Being